Why Me?

My fight for life from heartbreak to hope

First published 2019

This edition publisheded 2025 by Heartbreak to Hope Press,
an imprint of Heartbreak to Hope CIC, [London, UK]

ISBN printed book: 978-1-9191900-0-6
ISBN e-book: 978-1-9191900-1-3

Cover design by Sharon-Ann Phillips
Internal design by Andrew Easton

Why Me?

My fight for life from heartbreak to hope

SHARON-ANN PHILLIPS

Contents

Introduction

Why Me? is a long-awaited story, where I share my experiences and fears. Unveiling my passion and understanding, I provide insight into a journey of contradiction, love, determination and faith.

The pain of sickness and the sting of losing my loved ones challenged all my perceptions and, coming to a place of anguish and inactivity, I receive the motivation to impart my experiences.

Both my parents had died leaving me with so many unanswered questions. I needed to write 'Why me?' not only to record a fragment of a significant and crucial period in my life, but also to share of my experiences and my past. The first time my daughter had read a chapter of my unfinished manuscript, she exclaimed, "Wow, Mum, you actually had a life before us!"

"Yes, I had a life and still do," I responded. "With quite a few stories to share."

My desire to write started with poetry as a young person, in my early twenties, working in the City. Often writing numerous, poetic invitations and love letters on behalf of my colleagues.

A lifelong passion permitted me to start many stories, and

I always said there were so many different books in me. I did not get the opportunity to finish them as a single, working mother with three children to raise. However, I waited for the appointed time. Devastated by cancer and being laid off work, these life-changing events were the catalysts that finally triggered that passion to write a snippet of my story, in the hope of making a difference, having an impact and helping to change the lives of those who read it.

Marie, my elderly neighbour, was the first person who begged the question, "How could one person experience so much loss in such a short period of time and still have such faith?" A fair question frequently echoed by others, one that constantly resounded in my mind.

Claude, angry at my situation, with her tear-filled eyes and broken-heart, constantly asked, "Why you?" Birthed from those questions, came my story that tells how love, determination and belief can guide and help you through your world, even when all you see is darkness, sickness and death.

As I recall and pen the anguish, pain and trials suffered, my eyebrows are regularly knitted, my eyes frequently filled with tears. 'Why me?'

Foreword

It was an absolute pleasure to have been asked to write a foreword for Sharon's book 'Why Me?'; I know this will be the first of many.

Despite a shock diagnosis of a life-threatening illness, Sharon has transitioned to a fresh new place in her life. She has always been a bright, friendly, outgoing person; I have witnessed her newfound boldness, her increased faith and keen determination to share with others aspects of her life experience that will connect, encourage and bring hope and healing to others.

Her generous spirit and creative gifting combine to bring you the powerful story contained within these pages. The chapters reveal a young woman's personal account of her background and formative years, through to her unexpected collisions with tragedy and her parallel path to recovery.

As a close friend for the last two decades, I can attest to the veracity of this book, having celebrated with Sharon through seasons of joy and endeavoured to support through heartache and pain.

'Why me?' will encourage you to reach out to others, to do the good you can, while you can.

None of us knows what tomorrow will bring, so my hope is that if, or when, the unexpected happens in your life, like Sharon, you will turn to the living God and find Him to be faithful.

Dr Jacqueline McLeod

Chapter 1

FIRST REAL DIAGNOSIS

Answering the office phone, I knew immediately when the voice asked for 'Mrs Gayle' that the call was not associated with work. I had retained my maiden name for all work-related matters, so everyone still knew me as Sharon Phillips.

"Speaking," I answered. "How can I help?"

"Mrs Gayle, this is Chloe, I'm one of the consultants at St George's Hospital."

My heart sank and as a wave of panic swept through me, I promptly composed myself, so as not to alarm my nearby colleagues. We were in a large, luxury, open-plan office, where our Payroll and Benefits Department sat neatly within a cluster of four desks. There were five or six other accounts-related departments dotted around the room in the same format; I was aware that some colleagues would have been within earshot.

"Oh hello, Chloe," I replied, trying to sound casual.

"Mrs Gayle," she continued, "can you confirm your date of birth?"

Whispering clearly into the receiver and trying desperately to avoid attracting my colleagues' attention, I replied with my date of birth, making it sound as if it were a telephone or reference number. She thanked me then continued. "We've received the test results from your recent scan and it shows you have a rare condition." There was that awkward telephone pause before I calmly said, "Go on." Please don't give me bad news at work, I thought to myself as my tummy sank, at the same time willing her on to tell me what it was. "Only if you're sure it's a good time to go into it," she probed.

"Yes, go on," I replied again without thinking.

"The condition's called 'amyloid', I'll spell it for you: A-M-Y-L-O-I-D," she continued without taking a breath. "The cardiologist Dr Peters would like you to see her straight away, what's your availability?" she asked, oblivious to the fact that I was no longer listening; she then persistently rattled off a few dates. I was miles away. I dimly heard her urge me not to look it up until I had spoken to Dr Peters; however, I somehow managed to take her direct number and casually informed her that I would return her call.

With no idea what to expect and never having heard the word 'amyloid', ignoring her warning, I immediately put it straight into Google. As I read about the condition, the words 'fatal disease' and 'no cure' jumped out of the screen and resounded in my head. Surrounded by my colleagues, I needed to act normal.

"Just going for a coffee," I stated casually, excusing myself as I screen-locked my computer.

I knew there was something terribly wrong with me, but never expected an obscure name like amyloid. I sat on the toilet seat, head in hand, not really understanding what I had just read, but it made me weep. Maybe I should have felt reasonably satisfied, having been provided with a name at last after so long of not knowing what was happening to me, but I didn't; I would much rather have accepted and even believed the 'stress or anxiety theory'. After all, there hadn't been just one doctor who had mentioned emotional pressure, especially when I shared that our business was forced to close after four years.

It was 3:30 pm; I had an hour to go. I was now anxious to get home to Google more. I was consumed by a medley of emotions. After almost two years of ill health, there was finally a name, amyloid.

My travel home was one big blur. Although breezy outside, my unusually cold body seemed to be burning up inside. I carried my jacket over my arm. The old train station was just a few yards from work and upon seeing my colleague and usual travelling companion Laura at the train station, I avoided eye contact and made a diversion up the wooden stairs to the other end of the platform. I needed to be alone.

Once home I resumed my search. There was just so much information, too much information, but I needed to know before attempting to explain it to my family. Even then, I had no idea just how complex my condition really was.

It doesn't matter what age you are, when you hear devastating news, even at 51 you may as well be 15, you just want your mother. My husband Danny wasn't home. I thought about phoning him, but knew that if he was driving, he would take the call and that was not a good idea. We had been married for just over a year, although we had been together for almost six years.

Danny was easy-going, very calm and softly spoken. Tall, dark and handsome, with greying hair. We had met at a mutual friend's New Year's party in 2009. I was in tow with my three children and he came with his. We spoke in a group all night; in fact, Danny sat in the midst of the girls participating in our conversations, unbeknown to me at the time he was interested in seeing me again. This only came to light when he blocked my path, demanding my telephone number, as I tried to leave. I was not interested in a relationship and certainly not with a man with children so young (at the time his children were nine, five and four years old). I reluctantly gave him my number but had no desire to see him again. It was nine years since my fiancé had died and I lived alone with my children; I was quite contented and now very happy as a single mum.

We eventually had our first date, after my then boss, Karen, encouraged me to at least go out for a meal with him. We had so much in common, got along so well and apart from the usual step-parent issues haven't looked back since.

I knew he would be home soon and decided to wait until he arrived to tell him. In the meantime, I reached for my mobile and called Claude, my elder sister. She was at work and couldn't talk, "I'll call you back," she whispered down the phone.

At that point, it was seventeen years since our mother Cotcheta had died, and Claude had to some degree adopted the role of head of the family, even though she wasn't the eldest sibling. Claude was striking, over six feet tall and very attractive:

heads would turn when she walked into a room; she certainly had a presence. Three years my senior, she was medium-built and wore the most glorious wigs. She was always immaculately turned out. My 'Rottweiler', as most of my friends called her. She was so protective of her family and very passionate about anything concerning us.

It was 6:30 pm when she finally returned my call. "I'm on the train," she half-whispered in what we teased was her 'secret service' train voice. "What's up?"

"Claude?" I began. "Oh, just call when you're home, I need to speak to you." Apprehensively I hung up before she could question me and promptly continued my Google search. I wasn't sure how much information related to me, but it was all quite daunting.

My daughter Jess was in her room. She was seventeen, the youngest but most perceptive of my three children. She certainly had an inquisitive mind. I realised how clued-up she was, even at a very young age; she was no more than eight years old when she told me that the reason I was suffering from carsickness was because of the unbalanced fluid in my cochlea. She had obviously learnt about the ear and tried to piece together what my issues were; whether it was accurate or not, I had no idea, or inclination to check. I was very impressed with her conclusions and she continued to be our go-to person for any health-related or household issues. In a house with three men and me and Jess, it was Jess who would change things like the light bulbs or shower head, when needed. She was studying her final year of 'A' levels, whilst applying to do medicine at UCL, a career that was fitting and completely suited her supportive and helpful nature, as well as her intelligence.

Zack my eighteen-year-old, middle son was out, he was making 'beats' at his cousin Jermaine's house. He was very arty and creative; most of his childhood was spent with a pencil and paper, he was constantly drawing, usually DC Comics characters in some sort of combat. He had a passion for art and we always thought he would have taken his creativeness in art much further than the 'A' level stage; however, it seemed that he had a far greater passion for music and spent a great deal of his time in studios, or at radio stations. My eldest son Josh, who was 24 at the time, hadn't lived with us for a few months now, as he had moved out to be closer to his university.

Josh and Zack were like chalk and cheese. Josh was calm, kind, well-spoken and comfortable in any environment and circles. He was fairly quiet and never gave me cause for concern. We all said Zack had 'middle child syndrome', which mainly presented in him being more of a loner in the family. Although very loyal and trustworthy, he grew up more distant to Josh and Jess, who were very close to one another. Zack was certainly more streetwise than the others and often made us know it. Apart from his older cousin Dee, he did not spend much time with family and friends and certainly when we had the shop, where Josh and Jess were comfortably serving and helping out with customers, Zack stayed well away, as much as he could. Josh and Jess professed that he was the 'golden child' who regularly got his own way.

As a rule, growing up in our family, our parents seldom

shared anything with us and, although I was not ready to tell the children, I knew they deserved to know. Especially 'Dr Jess', who had supported me every step of the way through my illness. I knew she would be straight onto a search engine. There were just too many facts on the internet and I needed to know what related to me and make some sense of it all, before speaking to the children.

Chapter 2

LOSING VIV, MY ROCK

My late father, George Phillips, was a very humble man. He was handsome, tall and strapping, always in a suit and hat. His mother was a half-Indian Jamaican, and his father was white; whether he was a Jamaican, Syrian or English we have no idea, as he only met his father once, in his early years.

Primarily in the printing trade and an artist, he was known as 'Barber George', a name and profession he had inherited from his stepfather back in Jamaica. He had migrated to England in 1960, leaving my mother and eight children in Jamaica and immediately set up a barber chair in a room in Lewisham he rented from Mr Lawrence, a former migrant and friend whom he knew from Jamaica. We thought that Mr Lawrence was great because in the early 70s he worked for the BBC and had arranged for our family to feature in a television documentary about black families, called '24 Hours'.

George, or Papa G as we called him, soon became the local barber, where most of the black boys and men in Brockley, South-East London, went for their haircuts, or 'trims', as they would say.

Papa G, whose artistic talent knew no end, was also a

talented dancer, his speciality, tap-dancing. He shared many captivating stories of his time in Jamaica, of how he had won numerous competitions at the Ambassador Theatre and Majestic Theatre, back in uptown Kingston; alongside "Class performers, like Louise Bennett-Coverley," as he proudly put it. There were many days that he would show us all his skills and often teaching us girls to tap-dance, mainly me and my younger sisters, in the kitchen, whilst singing either Billie Holiday's 'All of Me', or Frank Sinatra's 'More'. He would pour salt on the kitchen floor to impact the sound of our shoes. It was exciting dancing with him. We thought he was the most sophisticated and talented dancer, who would have loved to be recognised for his brilliant talent. Sadly, the likes of *The X Factor* were not around in his day.

Both my parents grew up in a highly political Jamaica and were staunch People's National Party (PNP) followers. Mother worked in administration for the canvassers, whilst Papa G was involved in making and designing the party floats. He was a cartoonist for the newspaper who supported the PNP and often showed us pictures of the cartoon captions he used to draw for the newspaper, in Jamaica; his cartoons were humorous, with serious political messages.

His other hobbies were drawing and making models out of rubber moulds that he would set and fill with plaster of Paris.

Twelve months after Papa G had arrived in England, he sent for my mother and Claude, their youngest child, who at the time was just eighteen months old. It would take them another two years of saving before they could afford to send for some of the older siblings that had been left behind. Polly, Viv and Mike arrived in 1964 (by which time Juliet and myself were born); fifteen-year-old Jenny also came later that year. Pat and Joan were instead offered a great opportunity (or so my parents thought) and went straight to the USA to live with Papa G's aunt.

Twelve-year-old Audrey was the last sibling to leave her grandmother to join us in the UK in 1970. By the time she arrived, the family had extended significantly. Elaine and Paul were born in the late-60s and made the final number of children twelve. Being the first British-born sibling, I was born in St. Alfege's hospital in Greenwich, London, whilst my three younger siblings were all born at Lewisham hospital. It was no surprise that Papa G needed to work at three jobs; how he found time for his numerous hobbies, the pub and maintaining the home was a mystery. After leaving a bookshop on Upper Brockley Road, in Brockley, he started a new job in Great Russell Street; his main job was working as a curator in the Ancient Egypt Department, at the British Museum, and as a union member, also afforded the privilege of working night shifts, as a printer at *The Sun* newspaper, in London's Fleet Street. When he was not working nights, he would cut hair, in the attic most weekends and evenings, in our five-bedroom family home, which they had purchased in the mid-60s.

A very loving father and husband, our childhood memories of Papa G were numerous, with no two days the same. He showered us with love, especially his daughters. Every Christmas, for the employees' children, the British Museum would put on a pantomime and get Father Christmas to give presents to us all. I must have been about ten years old when I received my treasured nurses' costume complete with an upside-down watch and plastic stethoscope; that year my sister Juliet had received a Spirograph drawing set, with little cogs that you could draw around to make patterns with; she begged me to swap, but I loved my outfit too much and everyone said it fitted me just right. As children, the toys and presents from the museum were our Christmas highlights. With so many children in our household, our only Christmas presents from our parents were clothes and shoes, which we would wear on Christmas Day; so our real, fun presents came from the British Museum, year after year, up until Papa G's retirement in the early 80s.

The death of my sister Viv in 1996 came with overwhelming grief, leaving me shocked and numb. Until that day, it was evident I knew nothing about the pain of loss. My world shattered that day. My dearest friend and sister was gone forever. Up until that day I thought that I had grieved for my Aunt Ivy, or even my grandmother, when they died; but I really did not know what loss was. Watching my mother grieve added to the pain, we all said: she took it so badly, no one would have believed that she had eleven other children, but all she ever said was, "You don't expect to bury your child." Days later, I wrote a poem called, 'A parent outliving a child'. We were equally distraught and recognised that, although there were twelve of us, with different relationships, losing one was still very painful.

22 years later, I'm unable to think about Viv without pangs

in my heart.

I was eight months pregnant and at home with my six-year-old son Josh, when I received a call from my father asking me if I was ok, and if I was coming down.

"No, Papa G, it's Sunday, Josh has school tomorrow, I'm just settling him in for the evening."

"Alright," he answered. "We're home if you change your mind." We said our goodbyes and hung up.

As I reflected on the call, I wondered whether he had sounded rather sombre. I certainly heard a disappointment in his voice, and thought that's nice, Papa G still misses me, even in my thirties. I thought nothing more of it until Claude called twenty minutes later. "What you up to?" she asked. "Nothing why, what's wrong?"

"Just thought we would come over to you," she retorted. "Just checking you're at home."

"I'm home, you've called 'the landline,'" I said jokingly. "See you shortly, then," we said together as we hung up.

Claude lived about 9 miles away in Brockley, close to the rest of the family. Apart from our eldest sister Jenny who lived in Buckinghamshire and my three other sisters in the USA, I was the only sibling in the UK who lived miles away in Croydon. It was 7:30 pm, it would take her 40 minutes to get to me, which made me question why she would be coming so late on a Sunday evening. Surely she had work tomorrow. She would have spent most of the day cooking her traditional Sunday dinner, relaxed with the family, and would normally be preparing the children for school the next day. This was uncharacteristic and led me to question my father's earlier phone call. The house was untidy, Josh had his cars and toys everywhere, so I thought I'd better clean up a bit before she arrived; she didn't drive so I assumed her husband, Leroy, would be bringing her. I was clearing up when a wave of panic engulfed me: I instinctively felt that something was terribly wrong, I tried to ignore the feelings, but there was a pain deep within my gut.

After much deliberation, I picked up the phone and called my parents. My youngest brother Paul answered the phone. "Hi, Sharon."

"I want to speak to Mummy right now," I demanded, thinking that something had happened to her.

"It's not Mummy, Sharon, it's Viv," he said. "There was an accident."

"What kind of accident?" I interrupted before he could finish his sentence.

"A car crash, Vern and the children survived, Viv didn't."

"Viv didn't what, what do you mean? I spoke to her yesterday, she's fine, isn't she?"

"She didn't survive, Shaz."

"Nooooo….!" I screamed, dropping the receiver as I collapsed to the floor. The next thing I recalled was my friend, Dr Jacky, and Claude trying to get me to take deep breaths. Unfortunately, Paul was unaware that, due to me being pregnant, nobody wanted to give me that devastating news over the phone, for obvious reasons. Thankfully Claude had insisted on bringing Dr Jacky with her and they arrived promptly as I sank to the floor. Josh had been able to stand on a chair to answer the intercom and let them in.

"Who told you, who told you?" stormed Claude, tears of anger and disappointment streaming down her face.

"Paul," I whispered, in between sobs.

"That Mummy's boy is a blasted idiot!" she screamed.

"Claude, he's obviously in shock and not thinking," retorted Dr Jacky reassuringly and patting her on the back.

How could this be? Viv was my rock; we shared so much together and were so close; she did everything in her power to make all my dreams come true. She was one of those people, ahead of her time, who knew what action to take in every situation. She was talented, and so loved.

Viv was beautiful, immaculately turned out: she would spend hours each morning putting on her make-up, although we all knew she did not need any. She was married in London, age seventeen, to Brian Clarke, a German musician in a rock group called Black Velvet, whom she had fallen deeply in love with after frequenting his gigs. I cannot get my head around how my parents allowed her to marry at that age, especially as it transpired that he was an alcoholic and a 'wife-beater'. At 21, in an effort to escape the abusive marriage, she ran away to America, first to New York, then New Jersey, then back to New York, where she worked and struggled for many years, until she, at last, received her 'green card,' found her vocation, in real estate, and finally resided in Wappingers Falls, Dutchess County.

I had her Chase Visa card in my purse. I immediately took it out, tried to smell it to see if there was any trace of her. I inhaled it over and over, with my eyes closed, trying to get some kind of aroma, until I almost passed out, there was not a tinge. She was the sister who made so many things happen in our lives. There is absolutely nothing she would not have done for me or any of our siblings and vice versa; she would have taken the coat off her back if we allowed her. I even went on honeymoon with her and Vern, to West Virginia, to assist with a couple of foster children that they had at the time.

We called her our very own 'Oprah'. She had high hopes for me and once tried to pair me up with Denzel Washington's brother, David Washington, who just happened to be her husband Vern's groomsman. Although we partnered each other in their bridal party, nothing came of her prearranged plan. On another occasion, when an ex-partner of mine was causing me problems, it was Viv who persuaded me to leave the UK and come and live with her in the USA.

We had had one of our frequent heart-to-hearts on the phone, where I had shared with her his recent escapades, and I was truly upset. She called me back an hour later and said, "There's a ticket at Gatwick Airport, leaving for JFK, New York, tomorrow, at 7 am," she began, then concluded, "you don't ever have to go back!" She was adamant and had purposed in her heart that I would never return to London. I left everything, all the contents of my flat were divided amongst family. I lasted less than a year in America, but spent an unforgettable time with her and her family, working for the American Red Cross, travelling throughout various states and cherishing every moment.

It was Viv who gave me her Chase bank card and said, "If ever you or Mummy need any money, just go draw it out." The doors she opened for me were endless. We shared everything, true unconditional love. A love so evident to all around, and probably the catalyst that sparked my platonic relationship with her husband Vern.

Vern was wonderful, I had never met a husband like him, he worshipped the ground Viv walked on and her family. He was kind and gracious. There was nothing he would not do for me. On one occasion, I had heard a song at a Christmas play, 'Christmas Shoes', which I fell in love with. Vern searched high and low and did not stop until he finally found and purchased the CD for me.

As I shrank to the floor, I held my face in disbelief, shaking my head from side to side, sobbing my heart out. My eyes stinging from the tears. Josh was lying across my pregnant tummy, trying to understand what was happening, Claude and Dr Jacky were either side, trying to console each other and me. To this day there is no word to describe the pain and void I feel about her death.

I needed to understand what had happened. I called Vern, but could not get through. We later found out that Vern had been driving that Sunday morning, when their car careered off the road, into a ravine, hit a tree on the passenger side, where Viv was sitting and she died at the scene. He had sustained some injury to his leg; her two girls aged six months and eight years were sitting in the back, both unhurt. It was exactly a year after Viv's death, to the day, that Princess Diana had also died in a car accident.

Claude knew that she would have to collect me with Dr

Jacky. It was my mother's sister, Aunt Ruby who had received the upsetting phone call from New York. There was no way she was able to tell our mother, so she had driven to Claude's and broken the news to her and Leroy. Claude in turn had told our parents and all our siblings had gathered at the family home.

Our parents were devastated, heartbroken. My mother was not able to handle this tragedy, she was crushed. Little did we know that this would be the trigger of her demise. She survived less than 24 months after Viv, and Papa G survived less than 21 months after our mother.

Chapter 3

SOMETHING'S TERRIBLY WRONG

Viv and Mum's absence on my wedding day was the biggest lifetime void. I had to muster up everything inside me to get through the day. I kept thinking about Mother's eloquent speech at Claude's wedding and wondered what she would have said at mine. I wore her gold bracelet as a point of contact for their presence in my heart on the day.

It was eighteen months before the diagnosis, around June 2014, a month before finally marrying the love of my life, that I first had a persistent cough and noticed a difference in my breathing and stamina.

I had always been very athletic, even from a primary school age; I captained and played in both the netball and rounders teams, ran in the national school's athletic teams, and as a young adult played softball for St. Quintin's in the City of London. I always enjoyed swimming and various fitness classes, boxercise and spinning being a consistent favourite; however, I noticed a slight decrease in my ability to keep up. Our wedding was planned for July and I had put a lot of my exasperation down to the stress of the wedding, so never gave it too much attention. At 50, as a first-time bride, we really wanted it to be a grand affair. Danny had always impressed me with his ability to make my dreams come true; there was nothing he couldn't pull off. We had both been through so much and knew we wanted to seal the deal in style. It certainly was a day to remember.

A few months after, in October 2014, it was evident that something was undoubtedly wrong. On the 2nd of October, me, Claude and Dr Jacky were travelling to Wembley by train to see a play. We were meeting up first for dinner at London Bridge and I was running late, but struggling to walk to the restaurant, I arrived out of breath and sweating profusely; they were already seated. I was late and made my apologies. After a hurried Chinese meal, with my heart racing and feeling somewhat breathless, I felt I could only walk slowly, so told them I'd go on ahead of them and meet them back at London Bridge station to continue the rest of our journey. After paying the bill, they soon caught up and, whilst walking, it became evident that I could not keep up with them. I was struggling to walk and breathe, let alone walk and talk simultaneously, and by the time we arrived at Wembley I was exhausted. The girls were concerned and made me promise to visit the doctor as soon as I could.

I visited the doctor that week, only to be told that I was likely to be suffering from stress. Within days, I was struggling to walk again and experienced some tightness in my chest, this time I was with Jess and she insisted that we went to A & E in Croydon. The doctors immediately performed an ECG and took blood. I was admitted to hospital with Palpitations. The blood showed abnormalities in the heart and, although unexplained, they suggested I might have suffered a stroke or mini-heart attack. The doctors suspected some sort of coronary heart disease and decided to perform an angiogram; this procedure checked the arteries leading to my heart; I was warned of the potential complications but went ahead anyway. Under a local anaesthetic, a catheter was inserted into my groin, with a dye, which would show any abnormalities on the screen.

The doctors also performed an echocardiogram, a kind of scan that would take images of my heart. Over the course of those five days in the hospital, I underwent a series of various tests, which, apart from the raised enzymes in the blood, had all returned negative. Yet when I was admitted the abnormal blood count clearly gave a reason for concern. I was discharged none the wiser, with no diagnosis or medication. Dr Jacky had asked the consultant at the time to perform an MRI scan, but his response was, "That won't be necessary!" Those words still resound in my ears. In hindsight, I now believe the blood showed abnormalities due to the amyloid, which at that time remained undetected until the 'unnecessary' MRI scan was performed almost a year later.

Following my discharge from the hospital, I continued to experience breathlessness. I managed the situation silently, although when I travelled to Mexico with the girls, in February 2015, four months later, whilst sharing a hotel room and in close proximity with everyone, it became more apparent to us all that I was struggling to keep up. The contrast with my 50th birthday holiday, in the Dominican Republic, sixteen months before, was immeasurable. Claude, my sister-in-law Gina, my cousin Jackie, Dr Jacky, my niece Michelle, best friend Angie, her daughter Koral and Gina's husband Paul (who did not realise that he would be the only man) all came to celebrate with me. We had a fantastic time: my days were jam-packed. A typical day would see me up at dawn, in the gym, the first in the pool, aqua-aerobic classes, archery, salsa dancing classes, rifle shooting and any water sport going. Everyone commented that they were worn out just by watching me. Yet I presented totally opposite in Mexico.

On my return, I became extremely ill. I was overdosing on painkillers in an attempt to ease an excruciating pain, which I was suffering from in my upper torso. Feeling I was being stabbed all over and coupled with the breathlessness and pain, I went to see my doctor. I also had a nasty rash on my left torso, which needed some investigation. My doctor again put it all down to stress and anxiety; she felt that since I had experienced an admission at the hospital and they could not find anything wrong, then I must be stressed out about the recent closure of our restaurant. She told me to watch the rash and if it got worse, I should return.

By the following day, I was rushed to the hospital, the pain had intensified, again they performed the usual emergency tests and again there was a slight abnormality that kept showing up in the blood, giving the medics cause for concern, but yet again they found nothing specific. I was admitted and kept in overnight for observation, discharged the following day, again with no diagnosis or medication. Still in pain, a few days after discharge, my niece Michelle, who is an anaesthetist, came to visit; she looked at the rash and said, "Auntie, that looks like the viral disease shingles." I immediately turned to the internet process, analysing my symptoms and, sure enough, I had shingles, which attacked my left torso's side nerve. I went to the doctors and this time she acknowledged that it was, in fact, shingles, however, it was now too late for any medication, and I just had to let it take its course. I later found out that shingles is quite common with some forms of cancer.

Danny was working extremely hard; I assisted him whenever I could, working through the pain. His commute to Oxford was not easy. Every Thursday evening, I would set up a food stall, to sell a variety of food at the Hootannay Bar, in Brixton. I would cook the rice and peas, spicy jerk sauce and salads at home. Then take it all with the marinated chicken, Pattie warmers, equipment and utensils to the venue, where I would set up the large Jerk pan and stall, ready for the revellers who came to enjoy the live music and dancing.

I also started a new job in March 2015, as Benefits and Payroll Coordinator for a construction company in Surrey. This meant that I needed to commute by bus and train. It was a simple enough journey, as I was travelling against the flow of most commuters, who travelled into London. After a few days in the office, I realised that the cough became more frequent and my voice would become croaky, it was quite embarrassing and left me feeling vulnerable. I kept putting it down to the air conditioning, but it came and went without notice, not sure what my colleagues were thinking, but it made me feel very unprofessional. My next struggle was the flight of stairs that went up to my office. Once I arrived at work, if I took those stairs, by the time I reached my office door I felt the most peculiar, unfamiliar sensation all over my body. It was an unusual, weird feeling of tiredness coupled with an uncomfortable breathlessness, where I needed to catch my breath. On some occasions I'd be sweating profusely.

There was a lift, which no one but servicemen with equipment used; however, I decided I had to start using it to manage the breathlessness, even with the prospect of appearing lazy.

It was some months later that two things struck me. First, I was now struggling to walk a hundred yards, up my road, which had a slight gradient; and second, when I crossed over platforms at the train station, I could not walk the length of the train to sit in the carriage I required; I had no stamina and no ability for exertion whatsoever.

By June, I was phoning my children to meet me at the end of the road, to literally push me up it; I could hardly put one foot in front of the other. My legs persistently ached, almost as if running out of steam, and my tight chest was frequently pounding. I had no energy. Eventually I decided I had no option but to drive my car to the bottom of my road, so I could drive to our house when returning home, as this short, three-minute walk was no longer doable. The commute to work was a struggle and seemed increasingly unbearable. We used to laugh and say how easy it was for us to hear the bus coming and run to the bus stop all the way from home; now I was incapable of just running across the road to catch the bus.

I silently acknowledged that the effects of stress, as the doctors repetitively inferred, could not be the source of such compelling restrictions. Whilst I was still under the care of my local hospital, stress was nonetheless the only diagnosis, yet whatever my condition, it was apparent that my health was certainly deteriorating.

Chapter 4

A FRIEND WHO STICKS CLOSER THAN A SISTER

Dr Jacky came to visit me one day. She sat me down and passionately declared, "Shaz, I'm not at all happy with your breathing." She had that look which said, 'I feel there's something seriously wrong', but instead she added, "I think you should get yourself referred to another hospital straight away; there's a system called the choose and book, where you get your GP to refer you to any hospital of your choice. St George's Hospital in Tooting is very good, they have a great reputation there." Dr Jacky was the friend that God had somehow put in my life, always there at significant times. Most importantly, she came into my life a year before I lost my sister.

Dr Jacky was young, in her late-twenties when we first met, and only the second black doctor we knew personally. She was slender, sporty, of medium height with long, dark brown, wavy hair. She looked too young to be such a qualified and experienced GP. She knew her stuff and made us proud. When Claude introduced me to her in 1995, I was working locally, in the government buildings across from Lunar House, in Croydon, as a consultant for the civil service, recharging payroll costs and expenses for various government secondees all over England. With this job came access to a gym and squash courts, and Jacky and I would frequently play squash together, at least until I became pregnant with Zack. The minute she gave her recommendations, I immediately recalled how she had saved his life when he was only two years old, again when he was three, and ever since she made Zack feel like she was his own personal GP.

Shortly after Zack was born he developed eczema, where he was regularly wrapped in wet bandages; he had severe asthma and various allergies, his diet mainly consisted of Weetabix with soya milk or bananas; it's no wonder since his teenage years he never went near or touched bananas again.

I found out he was lactose intolerant at birth, as he would vomit every time he had my breast milk, so breastfeeding was not an option for him. We tried other baby-friendly milk until the doctors and I deduced that soya milk was the only one he was not allergic to; however, most of the other allergies I found out later, accidentally, the hard way. For instance, one afternoon, just after his second birthday, I decided I would try him with fish fingers. After just the second spoonful, he started heaving, as if going to be sick; this action was immediately followed by an inflammation of hives on his neck and chest. This, in turn, started to affect his throat; his neck had instantly started to swell up like a mushroom, making him gasp for breath. It happened so suddenly. However, impulsively Dr Jacky snatched him, grabbed the antihistamine from the cupboard and to this day (he's now in his twenties) I have no idea how much she actually gave him, as simultaneously she was screaming at me to get his

Ventolin inhaler. After what seemed like ages for me to locate it and hand it to her, she proceeded to administer at least ten puffs into the tube and into his mouth, whilst telling me to call an ambulance. His whole body looked very much like a Dunlop Michelin man. That was my first experience of seeing an anaphylactic reaction.

Dr Jacky was there again the second time it occurred, but on this occasion his allergic reaction was triggered by just the smell of fish; I was in the midst of boiling salt fish to make a traditional Jamaican dish of Ackee and Saltfish. I had no idea that an allergic reaction could be triggered purely by the smell of the culprit. It was similar to him having eaten the fish fingers yet again, but this time the allergic reaction seemed worse, it affected him with a vengeance, almost as if it had seeped into his bloodstream, and he was itching and writhing in pain as he went into the anaphylactic shock. She dealt with him in pretty much the same way as she had the first time; again, I believe she saved his life. It was no surprise that Dr Jacky was with us the third time he had a serious allergic reaction, or rather we were with her. I had taken the children on holiday to visit her in Boston, Massachusetts, whilst she was studying for her Master's degree at Harvard University.

We had naively or selfishly chosen to book dinner in a seafood restaurant one evening, which looked too good to pass. We assumed that warning the chef about his allergies and insisting that they use separate oils would be enough for us to have our lobster and prawn delights, whilst he enjoyed a nice dinner of chicken nuggets and chips. How wrong we were, unaware to this day what the chef's process was, however, once again fish triggered his allergic reaction. By this time, Zack (now nine years old) was prescribed an EpiPen, which he would carry at all times; however, on this occasion, it this was left in the apartment. He started gasping for air, vomiting and wheezing and all over his body started breaking out in hives. The scariest thing is seeing your child going into an anaphylactic shock. I was panicking, hopping around the restaurant in disbelief and unable to watch. Dr Jacky remained calm, took over the situation, did what she could, but ended up ordering the waiter to call the paramedics. Again, the antihistamine and inhaler assisted until the paramedics arrived, who boosted the medication, and after a few minutes (seemed much longer) normality began to creep in and he was able to breathe comfortably again.

God knows with all Zack's allergies and various health issues Dr Jacky has been instrumental and, to this day, we certainly value her constant input.

Chapter 5

ALARM BELLS RINGING

In June 2015 Danny's dear mother, Euphemia, whom we affectionately called 'Ma', sadly passed away at her home in Jamaica; he and his siblings travelled to bury her. I was unable to go with them, due to work commitments and I really was not feeling up to the journey anyway. Although I had never met Ma, we frequently communicated by 'Skype'. Ma lovingly called me 'The Queen'. She was a wonderful, fine, upstanding lady, whom Danny loved dearly and had great conversations with. Danny once asked me how I would describe her and I replied, "For an 80-something-year-old, she is with it and has certainly moved with the times. She was not judgemental and very kind." Danny laughed in wonderment as he agreed with my assumptions. I needed to support Danny as best I could and whilst the attention was on him, it was another distraction from my ill-health.

I was unaware of the choose and book system; however, decided to look into it. It was a couple of months before my dire condition forced me to finally take Dr Jacky's advice.

By mid-August 2015, through my GP, an appointment had been booked for me to see a cardiology consultant, at

St George's Hospital in Tooting. This hospital was at least 40 minutes away and I drove there with my sister Audrey, who insisted on accompanying me.

The consultant introduced himself simply as Jonathan. The meeting was intense, he asked loads of questions and for the first time I felt as if a professional was actually listening. He mentioned that alarm bells were ringing straight away with him, as he had observed that I had gone from being a usually fit 51-year-old, regularly at the gym, swimming and enjoying dancing, to barely able to climb a flight of stairs, or walk any distance without getting a shortness of breath. He was very thorough in his examinations and explained in great detail that he would organise a series of tests, pulmonary and cardiovascular simultaneously. He immediately booked an MRI scan and CT scan that he explained would take images of my heart and lungs, respectively, and insisted that other tests would follow.

Within weeks of the initial appointment, I had an MRI scan and it was this scan that revealed the abnormalities within my heart, which led to Dr Peters, the consultant cardiologist, recognising the traits of the rare disease, amyloidosis. Apparently, due to its rarity, most doctors would not have encountered a patient with amyloid in their lifetime, although they may have delved into it through their training.

After our initial contact, Chloe continued to communicate with me, she encouraged and updated me every step of the way. By the 1st of October 2015, I received a letter from her informing me that I had been referred to the National

Amyloidosis Centre, at the Royal Free Hospital, in Hampstead, North-West London, a division of UCL, who subsequently also wrote to me with an appointment for the 15th of October. It all sounded so critical and official; they even sent me a gallon bottle prior to the appointment, for me to bring a 24-hour urine test on the day.

The extent of my illness was concealed from everyone at work; it proved particularly difficult to get time off, and I now had to take two days off to collect the sample at home, without interruption. I decided against sharing what was going on with my manager, Katherine. She was too peculiar and I certainly would not get any sympathy from her.

On the morning of the 15th, UCL Royal Free Hospital sent a car for me, at 8 am, from their Q8 minicab, a special transport service run for patients; I arrived just in time for my appointment at 10.00 am. I was poorly and grouchy, the long car journey left me carsick, feeling awful and quite hazy.

I had justified going on my own, saying it was two hours away and just more tests, an all-day process, and I did not want to waste anyone's time. Danny didn't need much convincing as he was pretty consumed with his business and gave me my space, but, true to form, Claude and Dr Jacky travelled up by train to the hospital and met me in the afternoon. It really was an all-day appointment, full of various tests, an MRI, SAP & DPD scans. Both SAP and DPD scans consisted of me having a blue radioactive dye injected into my wrist, to assist with the investigation. It was painless enough, just a slight sensation as it travelled through my veins, but this meant that the DPD scan which was sensitive to detecting amyloid in the heart, would pick it up and the SAP scan, which could not detect amyloidosis or provide adequate information for moving organs, such as the heart, could detect the amyloidosis anywhere else in the body.

I was required to wait over two hours for the radioactive dye to circulate in my body before they performed the scan. Once the scans were done, I waited a further two hours for an appointment with the consultant. Claude and Dr Jacky had timed it well because this was when I needed my sister and friend more than ever. The consultant confirmed St George's amyloid findings; however, he went on to explain that there were two different main causes of amyloid, hereditary or cancerous. Doctors have a way of saying things in such a calm way, that even when you feel like screaming inside, you can remain dignified and composed. I felt like screaming! We all hoped for the amyloid to be congenital, but deep down knew that all possibility of this was remote. If the amyloids had been inherited, surely it would have been detected at a younger age; almost as if reading our thoughts, the consultant reassured us that he would not rule anything out at this stage as a minor procedure would show if it was hereditary or not, and the results could be ready the following day.

"I can take a tissue sample from your abdominal area, and this fat test would determine if a family member ever had amyloids," he added, trying to sound reassuring.

Of course, I agreed straight away and jokingly invited him to take as much fat as he possibly could.

The procedure was straightforward. Using a topical

anaesthetic, he numbed the surface of my skin and proceeded to syringe a small sample of fat from my tummy. It sounded worse than it was; I hardly felt any pain and he completed the entire process within seconds.

As I dressed, I could hear Dr Jacky ask him a few medical-related questions that, although he answered logically for her, went straight over my head.

As we left the ward, the consultant gave me his card and asked me to call him after 5 pm the next day.

We all promptly left the hospital and travelled the two-hour drive, back home in the Q8 minicab, the conversations a complete blur.

Chapter 6

NOT GREAT NEWS

The next day was Friday. I arrived at work as usual and thanked God that I had a strange ability to separate my personal life from my work life; it was uncanny.

That morning, unable to share what I was going through with colleagues, I eagerly worked in a beaver-like fashion, in an invariable effort to quickly get through the day. I almost chuckled to myself, like a madwoman, as I recalled all those many years before when, just 23 years old, I had walked into my flat to find the floorboards were bare and to the realisation that my then partner had completely stripped my studio flat, right down to the carpet. We had had a disagreement, (an understatement) and after telling him to leave, he did, taking all I possessed along with him. I was not expecting this extreme reaction. Distraught, I had gotten up, burning with pain and wounded inside, went to my job in the city, as if nothing had occurred. And now here I was once more, laughing with colleagues and acting as if I was living a glorious life and all was well, when in reality within the next eight hours I would know whether or not I had cancer.

I was being torn apart on the inside. Every so often I caught myself with my hand on jaw, watering eyes and a long sigh in disbelief of what I was experiencing. I felt so alone, my heart intermittently sinking throughout the day, as I clearly hid my grief and secret well. I had no plans to explain any of this to work colleagues and certainly not to my boss, Katherine, who sadly did not display any sympathy or empathy and remained quite impersonal most of the time. She was only four feet tall, yet easily weighed sixteen stones and walked like thunder. I never knew a boss like her and I had had a few, most of whom are lifelong friends.

On the one hand, Katherine was very talkative, my interview, which was conducted solely between the two of us, had lasted over two hours and she had employed me on the spot. Yet most mornings she would walk into the open-plan office in a foul mood and completely ignore everyone in her path, not even a 'Good morning' until such time as she was ready to talk. The way she treated me seemed heartless; my employment was on a temporary to permanent basis, where a permanent job would be offered to me after three months of proving myself capable in the role.

After the first month of employment, it was evident through my performance that I was more than qualified to undertake the role. At this stage in my life, payroll was a doddle to me, I was familiar with the many changing procedures and software. In fact, in the very first month I had single-handedly reduced the weekly payroll inaccuracies from 75% to 15%. A few of my colleagues commented that my work ethic was great; there were evident changes since I commenced and there was no financial reason for a growing company with a group turnover of over

£1.5 billion not to take me on permanently. However, it was Katherine's decision and she, although admitting how pleased she was with my performance, kept moving the goalposts, with various excuses at the pivotal times.

My colleague Mary, who worked very closely with me, had become a close friend. She was Mauritian, with a lovely, kind persona, she looked great and much younger than her 62 years. She was hard-working and equally good at payroll. One afternoon, as we were finishing up at our desks, she received a personal call on her mobile. I could see she felt awkward about it, as she walked out of the office to conclude her call. I later found out that the call was from her employment agency, who had called to inform her that the company no longer required her services and her contract would end in three weeks.

Yet Katherine sat opposite us both in the office for those three weeks, until the day Mary left, without mentioning a word to her that she no longer required her, whilst setting up a replacement behind her back. Her managerial practices seemed harsh and unconventional, her motives certainly questionable.

If Mary had still been there, I would have had a confidante to speak to, but she wasn't.

Katherine had lost her five-year-old daughter through a sudden illness three years before I started and understandably this evidently affected her gravely; she seemed unemotional, somewhat stony and treated colleagues reservedly, which revealed an unwelcomed coldness. Although she chatted endlessly about her daughter, she behaved in an unprofessional manner and displayed no compassion towards the staff. I felt her pain, it was apparent that a part of her had died along with her daughter. I often reminded myself of the anguish she would undoubtedly be feeling, in a strange way, she just seemed to want everyone to be feeling her pain, too. There was no way I could share what I was experiencing with Katherine, I was not able to deal with any more hurt; I was myself between a rock and a very hard place.

We were extremely busy, as usual, Friday was payday for the weekly paid workers, and the phones were going non-stop with queries. I was grateful, there was no opportunity for small talk with my colleagues and, before I knew it, it was 4:30 and time to go home. Little did I know that that was to be my very last day with that company.

Claude had expressed how much she wanted to be at home with me when I called the consultant at 5 pm, but I knew I could not wait until she came. I arrived home just after 5:15 pm, searched my bag for my phone and as I reached for the card and dialled the mobile number, tears flooded my eyes and perpetually rolled down my face. I was standing in front of the mirror in the lounge observing my tears, as the male voice of the consultant answered my call and announced his name; my calm voice intently spoke, through the undetected tears. "Hello, it's Sharon Gayle, I've called for my results."

"Hi, Sharon, yes erm, Sharon, I was expecting your call," he proceeded awkwardly. "Can you please confirm your date of birth, just for data protection purposes."

With my beating heart feeling as if it was now in my throat, I paused, filled with emotion, tongue-tied: I could not find my voice.

"Sharon, are you there?" came the voice from the end of the phone.

"Yes, I'm here, sorry," I replied as I loosened the grip on the phone and systematically reeled off my date of birth.

"Ok, it's not great news." My heart skipped a beat, even though I could have completed his sentence, I was still in shock.

"I'm afraid we can deduce that the amyloid is not hereditary and therefore we are required to perform further tests to establish exactly where it stems from," he answered without taking a breath, then continued. "We will write to your consultant, Dr Peters at St George's and we will both be in touch to work out the next stage. If there's anything you need to know in the meantime, please don't hesitate to call me." I think I said, "Ok," as we said our goodbyes and hung up the phone.

Jess was first home, and when I reluctantly gave her the results, with tears in her eyes and delicately trying to remain strong, she quietly murmured, "I wanted it to be the hereditary one, I knew it wouldn't be. Are you ok, Mum?" I did not answer, a huge lump came up in my throat, I had no more words, no more tears, my palms were sweating and I was breaking down internally. I held her tightly, a reassuring embrace which said don't worry, it will be ok. Secretly I was in two minds about the results: if it was hereditary, then surely my children could inherit it and I would never have wanted that.

"Where's Danny?" demanded Claude, the minute she walked through the door and I gave her the results. "He should be here!" she insisted. I could tell she was biting her tongue;

then she proceeded to give me a hug, holding me close to her bosom and kissing me on the forehead.

We all knew that she thought Danny was not paying enough attention to what was going on with me, yet frankly he was dealing with it as best he could and I knew he was a bit oblivious of the situation and somewhat in denial.

The first time Claude and Dr Jacky had met Danny, I was left embarrassed and very disappointed. It was supposed to be a nice introductory meal, at my favourite Thai restaurant in Crystal Palace, and equal distance from us all.

After asking Danny what his intentions were with her sister, she proceeded to ask him, “Who chopped you in your head, then, Danny?” referring to an aged scar. Thankfully Danny remained polite; but the tone of the meal was set, with her other prying questions. She continued to inform him, her tone quite firm, that I had no mother and she had assumed our mother’s role, by looking out for me and making sure no one took advantage. I have no recollection about the food, but the evening was a disaster. I was not happy with my sister’s frequent bluntness and left feeling that I had walked Danny into a lion’s den.

Throughout my illness, Claude had Dr Jacky every step of the way and I knew that, without a doubt, Dr Jacky would have been giving her the specifics of what was really going on with me.

Zack arrived home just as Danny was pulling up. We told them both at the same time. Zack did not say a word; we wondered whether he understood what we were saying. We all thought if it’s not hereditary, it must stem from cancer, but no one said it. Zack was probably the only one who hadn't worked it out. As I looked into his eyes, he seemed vague, almost subdued, even non-committal, as if he had blocked out everything he had just heard. He brought me right back to the day his father Phil Linton had died, fifteen years before, Zack was only four years old and it happened on our daughter Jess's third birthday, a birthday we would never forget. Phil was a talented singer, songwriter and producer, who had written songs for James Ingram, Patti Austin, Maxi Priest, Soul II Soul and numerous other artists. He had just signed a singles deal with a song he had written and produced, with Basement Jaxx, called 'Don't Stop'; sadly he died within a few months of its release at 38 years old, from a perforated ulcer, in 2000 the same year of my father's death. It was a shock to us all; the professionals all said, "You do not die from perforated ulcers in this day and age," and that was so true. Only Phil had a deep fear of hospitals and once admitted, he discharged himself purely through that fear. It was the underlying fear of hospitals which ultimately prevented him getting treatment and subsequently killed him.

We always said that Zack's grief and loss were never really dealt with, suppressed and internalised and that's how he had learnt to deal with distress, from then until now; unlike Jess, who wanted no stones unturned. It was pointless discussing it any further with him; I knew he had heard as much as he wanted to hear for the night.

Danny had hung his head, with his lips clenched tightly together in a straight line; I could see the tears in his eyes.

Please do not cry, I silently pleaded with him from deep inside me. As if reading my thoughts, he came over, squeezed me tightly to him and promptly asked if anyone wanted a cup of tea, took orders and swiftly scampered into the kitchen.

The next few weeks were crucial. The hospital called me in for blood tests and a 24-hour urine test; they hadn't mentioned cancer at this stage and Google was playing havoc with my emotions.

The hospital letters were coming in thick and fast. November the 5th was the day booked for me to take a bone marrow biopsy, this was the test they required to confirm where the amyloid was stemming from. Claude accompanied me to the appointment and I knew it was not an easy procedure; Dr Jacky had warned me about potential complications and pain, which were substantiated when they asked me to sign the disclaimer and reeled off a list of side effects.

I also knew a couple of friends who had previously had bone marrow biopsies and told me about the pain. Drilling through my bone, into my bone marrow, pinching a piece of the bone marrow flesh and then a piece of the bone was neither easy nor pain-free. I was writhing in pain and left in tears.

Chapter 7

NO TIME TO WASTE

My next appointment was to see the consultant cardiologist, Dr Peters, on the 10th of November 2015. Claude was unable to be present for the appointment and begged me not to attend alone. "Shaz, I'm serious," she said sternly. "Let Danny go with you or ask one of your friends, just don't go to that appointment on your own." I had not asked Danny, as I knew he was working on a new project; he was in the process of closing his bakery in Oxfordshire, which was over two hours' drive away and opening up a new Caribbean restaurant near Brockwell Park.

I wasn't worried about seeing the consultant alone and, although usually quite stubborn, on this occasion I obediently asked my friend Sophia to attend. Sophia had been one of my five bridesmaids; she had suffered a life-changing brain haemorrhage a few years before, was off work and available. She was one of my friends who had asked, "Why you, Sharon?" and the kind of friend that would assist any way she could. Along with her confirmation to accompany me, she also messaged me and stated, "I wish I could extract your illness from you and put it in my body; that way you won't have to go through this. Illness has already compromised my physical and mental health, so a bit more will not hurt me. It would save you and yours from this journey." I was blown away and knew without a doubt that she meant every word of it.

Once in the appointment with Dr Peters, Sophia recorded the consultation. Thank God she was with me. It was here that Dr Peters explained that I was required to be admitted to St George's straight away, there was no time to waste and they were working tirelessly with the haematologists to confirm strategies for treatment. She clarified that my heart was extremely damaged. A heart transplant was not an option for me, as the abnormal proteins were kicking off in my body and would just attack the new heart; she explained and justified chemotherapy as the recommended option. Even without the results and confirmation of the biopsy, they determined at this stage that I would be required to have chemotherapy and there was no time to waste.

Chemotherapy did not sit well with our family at all. Mother had been 71 when she died. Up until her death, she was the glue that kept our nationwide family together. She was the life and soul of every party, most of which she planned herself. Our home was always full of visitors; they turned up in their droves, family and friends, often with a bottle under their arms. In the 60s they mainly drank VP wine and Long Life beer, and the spirits would be consumed in shot glasses. Later, whiskey and Smirnoff vodka became the favourite, often mixed with Tree Top orange squash. We grew up in a very traditional Jamaican home. Always a large pot of food cooking on the fire. We knew what dinner we would have each day. Thursdays were our favourite days, we would race home from school to watch *Little House on the Prairie* and knew that by the time we arrived at the bottom of our road, we would smell the sweet aroma of stew peas and rice cooking on the stove. It was cooked in the biggest pot, with brisket, pigtail, salt pork and salt beef; a dish big enough to feed the multitudes because everyone loved it. It was delicious and still a favourite of ours and many Jamaican families' to this day.

Mother, a trained hairdresser and seamstress, worked in a factory at Aldgate East in London's East End when she first arrived in Britain, sewing and ironing for a Jewish-owned business. In the 80s she worked as a cook at a main sorting and post office in Mount Pleasant, London's Farringdon; her shifts were 6 am until 2 pm, which meant she was always home when we returned from school. She would leave home by 5 each morning, our dog Bullet would walk her to the bus stop, wait for the bus then make his way back home, where Papa G or whoever was up first would let him in.

Mother retired at 65 and had always been very active, travelling and enjoying her life, so her death came as a big surprise and was certainly unexpected. She had been diagnosed with lung cancer, gone into hospital for a routine dose of chemotherapy, got very distressed under the treatment, and died within hours. Whilst we acknowledged that lung cancer was her diagnosis, nothing could have prepared us for this. The doctors had been optimistic and, when diagnosed, informed us that although terminal, she would live in excess of two years; little did we know it would only have been less than six months.

No one could have agreed more that she was one heck of a tough woman. Having given birth to twelve children, and worked most of her life, whether pregnant or not, she was the strongest woman I had ever known. She wore the trousers in our home and often gave Papa G a tongue-lashing, especially if he came home drunk from the pub. She was fun and funny, a practical joker, mischievous, with a great sense of humour. She would find it hilarious frightening us; apart from the scary songs she would sing, she would put a stuffed toy rat on a see-through string and pull it past us, or she would put a rubber spider on your shoulder and make you turn around, then laugh at you squealing in fright.

Sometimes when we knew she was listening outside our bedroom door (the stairs in our home creaked terribly, so we always knew when anyone was outside), we would recite in unison a poem that I have no idea who taught us: 'I love my mother above all things, I love the way she talks and sings, I love the way she smiles at me, she's gentle, patient, sweet and kind, the nicest mother I could find.' She was rumbled and would end up coming in and we would all fall about laughing. She had a presence and everyone said she certainly kept the family and extended family together. We believed she would have conquered the cancer; in fact, the tumour was shrinking, it was the chemotherapy that actually killed her. Our family has never been the same.

When Mother died I had felt so guilty. I was the one scheduled to take her to the hospital that morning, yet, the night before, my sisters and I debated as to why it was always me despite the fact my children were the youngest. Eventually, Claude managed to persuade Audrey to accompany Mum this time. Little did we know that there would never be another opportunity.

There were so many questions; at the time, there were queries as to whether the nurse had taken her blood pressure or not; the thought never left me. If I had been with her, would I have been more perceptive and involved to notice? After all, it was only the day before that Claude and I were checking with the doctors whether she was actually strong enough to undergo another dose of chemotherapy. We thought differently and tried to persuade her against it; but she was so despondent, weary and disheartened, she went along with anything they said, never weighing up the consequences for herself. We believe she stopped caring and had already given up on life, since the day Viv died.

I recall the day she died as if it was yesterday. It has never left my mind. I was at home when the frantic call came, from Leroy, for me to go to the hospital; I was cooking lunch for my children and my nieces. I immediately called Phil, who was in the studio, to say I would drop the children to him, as I needed to get to the hospital to see my mother who had become distressed under the chemotherapy treatment. I drove to Guy's Hospital, which was over an hour away; had no idea how to get there (no sat nav in those days), but somehow after dropping the children off, God took hold of the wheel and I found my way. By the time I arrived at the car park, Claude was outside with Leroy, screaming at the top of her voice; the shrill of her screams have never left me. I had driven my white Toyota Camry and to this day I am not sure who parked my car; but as we held each other and walked towards the ward, all she kept saying in between her cries was, "She's gone, Shaz, she's gone."

I arrived at the ward to more screams and bawling. My siblings had already arrived and my eight-year-old niece Kira was lying on her grandmother, blowing into her mouth and screaming, "Grandma, have some of my breath, I've got more than enough for both of us." As if her death wasn't enough, seeing my little niece crying like this broke our heart. Mother was cold, stiff.

"Why had I not taken her to the hospital today?" I was mortified and riddled with guilt, and this guilt remained with me for many years.

Now here I was in Dr Peters' office being offered the same drug that had killed my mother all those years before.

She went on to explain that my admission now required great urgency, in fact within days. She expounded that, although the haematology department usually administers chemotherapy, it was necessary for my admittance to occur under the care and protection of the cardiology department, where a heart machine would be constantly attached to me, enabling my heart to undergo 24/7 monitoring.

Dr Peters spoke in very low tones. Sophia and I both looked at each other as she squeezed my hand reassuringly. I was relieved she was with me. Overwhelmed, tears flooded my eyes, as she offered more and more information and reality began to set in. This was a new world for me. I could not take it all in, so it made all the difference knowing that the meeting was being taped.

Dr Peters informed us that the result from the biopsy was due on the 12th of November and an appointment had already been made for me to see the consultant haematologist, Dr Willis, as soon as possible on the day.

Sophia and I left the hospital arm in arm, quiet and subdued.

The excerpt below is from the Jamaican Gleaner on Wednesday 30th of September 1998. Following the untimely passing of my dear mother

Jamaican community member passes away

The late Cotcheta Phillips

A PROMINENT member of the Jamaican community in South-East London, Mrs Cotcheta Maria Phillips (formerly Black), aged 71, was recently laid to rest at Grove Park Cemetery after a service conducted by Father Vincent at St Saviours Church in Lewisham, South-East London. She was the wife of George Phillips, and together they had 12 children, 28 grandchildren and eight great-grandchildren.

Her son, Michael Phillips, a well-known singer sang "God Be With You Till We Meet Again" and there were further renditions of poems, psalms and eulogy by relatives Ingrid Marsh (reading a poem written by Debbie Marsh), Elisha Charlton, Sandra Marsh and Shakira, Cerine and Joshua.

The late Mrs Phillips was born in Kingston, Jamaica and came to England to join her husband in 1961. A qualified hairdresser Cotcheta worked at the Post Office until she retired. She was undergoing treatment at Guy's Hospital for suspected cancer when she passed away. Cotcheta and George, and their large family were conspicuous in community social life, particularly in the 1960s and 1970s at which often she provided the catering. The deceased was a member of the United People's Social Benevolent Association No 1.

Chapter 8

THE CONFIRMATION

The morning of the 12th of November, I determined that I would not cry; I had no more tears. I would be strong; it was quite clear what the outcome would be. Danny made time and was determined to accompany me. Claude took a half-day from work; we picked her up a few roads from the hospital at Tooting train station and drove to the hospital for the consultation with Dr Willis.

As we waited in the reception, I could see Claude's mouth moving as she prayed under her breath. Danny tried to lighten the situation by telling me about the latest shenanigans at the shop. When the nurse called my name to go in, we all jumped and looked at each other. I gave a grim, lip-bitten smile and went in, as directed, to see the consultant; it was not Dr Willis, as previously assigned, but a Spanish consultant called Pedro. Pedro was tall, kind, olive-skinned and gorgeous, but it soon became apparent that he was not the ideal consultant for what was required. After the introductions, we waited anxiously and expectantly for Pedro to begin.

His tone was soft and he spoke hastily in a Spanish accent, with his diction often incorrect.

"So Sharon, my name is Pedro, one of the haematology doctors under Dr Willis, you've been seen by Dr Willis already?" I responded by saying, "No." He continued rather quickly. "She usually runs the clinic, but unfortunately is unable to meet with you today. We are three doctors here today that deal with the haematology; she told me that you have recently been diagnosed with amyloidosis, and in the heart, so we are going to admit you, you know that we are going to admit you, at the weekend. You know the plan already?"

"Yes, well, I was told yesterday that I was going to be admitted on Saturday," I replied, my voice shaky and quite squeaky. I sounded like a ten-year-old, but there was nothing I could do about it. "Is that right?" I enquired. Pedro responded with, "That's for sure, that's fine, that's fine. As long as you are admitted in the weekend. I'm not on at weekends so my colleagues will see you." Before he could go any further, Claude interrupted. "What did you say your name was again?"

"My name is Pedro, Pedro Badia, B-A-D-I-A," he replied, spelling out his surname. Claude repeated his name as she wrote it down.

"Anyway," he reassured, "we are carrying the bleep for the Haematology, so any problems they will let me know." I guessed he heard the directness in her solicitor's tone and wanted to let us know that he would be accountable.

"So have you been told about the disease and about, er, what does it mean and have we gone through the explanation of the amyloidosis?"

"Yes," I replied, nodding my head.

"So you know these things are being emitted from your bone marrow and depositing themselves into your heart, and you know that you are going to be admitted under the cardiologist?" he asked.

"Yes," I replied again.

At which point there was a knock on the door.

"Yes, come in!" shouted Pedro. A lady came in dressed in the navy blue Macmillan nurses' uniform.

"Hello, my name is Jo, I'm one of the Macmillan nurses," she announced as she introduced herself.

Everyone responded by saying, "Hello," in unison. This was the first time Danny had opened his mouth since entering the room.

"Who's Sharon?" asked Jo.

"I'm Sharon," I answered, whilst Claude simultaneously pointed me out.

"Hi, Sharon, nice to meet you, I see you've brought your family," Jo commented soothingly, as Claude introduced Danny and herself.

"I'll just sit at the back here," Jo continued as she sat behind us on the couch.

Pedro introduced her again as one of the specialist nurses. I guessed straight away that she was there to offer support and clarity. She was tall and slim, yet unassuming, with a very kind, soft voice. In fact, everyone's voices were soft, gentle and low-volume; mine was very quiet, childlike and trembling. Claude asked most of the questions and it wasn't until we were more than fifteen minutes into the conversations that the word 'cancer' actually emerged.

Danny and I sat next to each other in front of Pedro's desk, whilst Claude sat adjacent to us, a couple of seats to Danny's left.

"Jo will give you some of the information," added Pedro as he pointed to Jo, then continued without pause. "You're going to be admitted under the cardiologist, that's the safest ward for you to be under; they have something called monitoring. So they got all the patients to have a little label here." As he spoke, Pedro showed us the sticky heart labels.

"So we can check how the heart is working, so is the most safest ward to keep you in, ok?" His Spanish accent was even stronger the faster he spoke.

"Yes," I answered.

"We are going to give you chemotherapy, so you will be seen by haematology doctors every day. Ok? So although you're going to be under and monitored by Cardiology, you will be seen and monitored by us every day. Shared, they will check the heart and we will check everything else. Ok?"

"Sure, joint care," I answered. "I understand."

"So, erm, as soon as you come in we will check the bloods and start the chemotherapy on Monday. We can give you all the information today and we can give you the consent form to read over the weekend, or you can sign it today. Usually the patient signs this when they have been briefed about all the side effects of the chemo."

My mother flashed before me when he mentioned 'consent form', and my stomach turned over; Claude must have felt the same.

"So we are going to give you something called CVD, which means three medications."

"CBD?" Claude clarified as she wrote the letters down.

"No, CVD!" repeated Pedro.

Jo interjected at this point and said, "There's no need to remember this all or write all this information down, as it's too much, you will get everything in the pamphlet."

"Oh, ok," Claude responded, quite relieved.

Pedro handed me the pamphlet and said, "I'm going to explain it all now, but during the weekend you can have a look, ok? We are going to give you three different medications, ok? One is called cyclophosphamide, the other one is called Velcade or bortezomib, and the other one is dexamethasone, which is steroids, ok?"

He said 'ok' so many times that it started to irritate me and I silently wished he would stop.

He went on to explain the frequency, how the different medication would be administered, as well as the various dosages.

When Claude started taking notes again, Pedro explained that everything he was saying was in the pamphlet. Pedro then went on to break down all the cycles of the drug, at which stage Claude, ignoring the fact that it was all in the pamphlet, continued writing.

"We are going to give you 'one dose' and see how you respond, for one day, ok? Don't worry," he said, "I will write the cycles down for you."

"And will I be staying in hospital for all that treatment?" I asked.

"Yes," replied Pedro.

"Roughly how long?" I asked.

"For a few weeks."

"Two…two weeks?" asked Claude, stammering.

"No, a little bit more," corrected Pedro.

Jo then told us, "It's so that they can monitor you, after the medication; you will be attached to the heart machine. You see, with amyloidosis, after this type of drug, it can make you put on more fluid, which can shift things, so they monitor you very closely. And obviously everyone is different," she repeated, "so we wouldn't give you the Velcade and the cyclophosphamide probably on the same day so that we can see all the side effects. They will want you in so that we can keep a really close eye on you."

I could sense that she was picking her words very carefully, and detected the seriousness in her explanations.

Claude repeated again, "So it will take more than two weeks?"

"In the past, in my experience, it has been," Jo responded quite confidently.

"Ok," said Claude, nodding in appreciation of Jo's clarity. Jo continued. "But then we obviously do aim, our main aim is to get you home, allowing you to just come in to us as an outpatient. But sometimes we have to tweak it."

"So it depends on Sharon, basically," said Claude. Pedro then agreed. "Yes, it depends on the patient how they respond to the treatment, so there's not a fixed rule. We cannot say after fourteen days you can go home, it depends on how you and your heart are responding to all the treatment," he continued as he pointed to me.

Pedro continued to elaborate on the effects of the treatment and went into great detail around the immune system, speaking really fast; at one stage I wondered whether he was late for his next appointment. Claude relentlessly interrupted him to seek clarity every step of the way. At one point she stopped him mid-sentence and asked, "Side effects?"

At which point Pedro proceeded to list them all. "With the cyclophosphamide it's really common you can have nausea, you can have vomiting, you can have something called aplasia, which means that the bone marrow which is a factory of the blood can get like, but not completely destroyed, but it can be reduced, which means that you may need to have transfusion of red cells, transfusion of platelets and sometimes you need antibiotics, in case you have fever or infection, and sometimes..." before he could finish his sentence, Claude interrupted again. "Sorry, doctor, sorry, how often is that?"

"You mean the side effects? It depends on the patient," Pedro stated.

"Depends, ok," Claude said, acknowledging with a sigh.

Pedro continued directing his answers at Claude. "Her immune system is going to drop, she can develop an infection, but it depends, it depends".

"With the dexamethasone, the steroid, it usually produces, like you can develop insomnia, so what we usually do is give the steroids in the morning. So during the day you won't fall asleep and you can have a proper sleep during the night. It can also produce some problems with the heart because the amyloid is in there, ok, so you can have chest pains, you can have tightness, you can feel a bit dizzy, so that's the reason you will be admitted. And the Velcade can produce, erm, can make your platelets come down."

"Make the what?" said Claude.

"Platelets," repeated Pedro, "so the cells that are used to stop the bleeding, they can go down. You can also have, with the Velcade, some vomiting and diarrhoea; you can also have something called peripheral neuropathy, which means that you can feel like numbness and tingling, in your hands and feet." I finished off his sentence, as I had read about peripheral neuropathy. "Er, I think that generally speaking that's most of the side effects, everything is written here."

The conversation went on between Claude and Pedro for what seemed like hours, backwards and forwards. She left no stone unturned and he obliged as best he could.

He handed me another leaflet.

"What else?" he asked, almost asking himself.

"Would I be able to have visitors?" I asked.

"Yes," said Pedro. "It depends, as long as they do not have any colds or infections, as your immune system is low. We will monitor your immune system and in case it really drops, you may be put in a side room and people will be able to visit you."

With every side effect that Pedro revealed, I could hear Danny grumbling or sighing loudly, letting out deep moans in my ear.

I knew that Danny was not comfortable with me having

chemotherapy at all, especially now after hearing all the side effects, so after many minutes of him not saying a word, it was no wonder he asked, “Is it necessary to have the three different drugs?”

“Yes, because they have done trials and a lot of research, regarding the medications, and they think that it is better to have three medications rather than to have one or two, so it is better for the patient’s survival, so the patient will live longer. It is better for us to try and keep the disease under control, otherwise we wouldn’t give three. It is true that the more tablets we give, the more likely it is to have side effects, but it is also true that the more tablets, it has been proved is better for the patient, we get a better chance of attacking the disease.”

I asked Claude for my list. Dr Jacky had met up with me the night before and helped me draft a selection of relevant questions.

“Do I start on a low dose? Is that what would happen?” I asked, head down, as I scanned the list, realising that most of the questions we had compiled had already been covered.

Jo answered, “It’s a specific dose to start with first, there is an amyloid protocol, then if we need to increase, we would. We have a regime to start with, a tried and tested regime.”

Looking at my notes, I asked, “So you know you said it’s fighting the disease. I understand that it is stopping the disease from attacking my heart, is it actually stopping the amyloid as well, does it attack the amyloid that’s already there as well? So the other side of it, because I have not had the results from my bone marrow biopsy. So I need to know what’s going on there.”

Pedro responded by saying, “Hmm, yes, I can tell you.”

Claude then said, “So I thought this was what we came for today.”

To which Jo replied, “Yes definitely!”

There was a very long pause whilst Pedro turned to his computer and almost pretended to be looking up the results, instead of being specific; there just seemed to be a lot of waffling. It was obvious: why else was Jo, the specialist Macmillan nurse, invited? I guess it was all procedure and no one really wanted to confirm what we already knew. In fact, through conferring with other patients later, I found out that the consultants are excellent at giving your treatment plan and talking through the various procedures, discussed by the management teams, but actually saying, ‘You have cancer,’ does not come naturally.

A couple of minutes passed. It seemed much longer; I felt as if my breath had stopped.

“Yes, so they said that there is a...” As if changing his mind, Pedro paused, then continued. “The cells that usually produce the amyloid are called plasma cells, so there is an infiltration of the marrow, which means that the cells producing the amyloid are into the bone marrow, ok? What does that mean? It means that the cells that are producing the amyloid can get a start to any organ; in your case, it has attacked your heart. It means once we want to reach a stage, to check how the heart is doing, we check the cells and control the cells, with the chemo if it is working.”

Another long pause and then I asked, “What cells?”

I expected him to say the word ‘cancer’, but he still didn’t. He went into something else. “The plasma cells, the cells that I told you about, the plasma cells, the cells that produce the amyloid. The cells that are attached to the tissues, in your heart."

"So if we can control the cells, we can control the amyloid."

More waffling.

"So what's the problem with the cells? What's causing these bad cells to behave in this way, to attach to my heart?" I asked, voice quavering.

"The plasma cells, hmm, the plasma cells should not be in there, it's a kind of, so it's, erm, the plasma cells are a kind of tumour of the blood, it's, erm, a kind of tumour that is in the blood. That's produced. The cause, we don't know, well, not here, not any of the haematologists or research here know what's caused this kind of tumour. So we need to give you a treatment, so if the chemo is effective, it will mean that it will decrease the cells that are producing the amyloid. So if we stop the cells, growing, because they are growing more than they should." Pedro was stating the obvious and repeating himself.

I interjected, saying, "Yes, I understand that, it's quite clear."

Pedro continued to reiterate, talking more and more about the cells and the treatment.

Until Claude interrupted him again and asked, "So if you stop the plasma cells, obviously the amyloid will stop?"

"Yes," answered Pedro.

"You said tumour, Pedro, you used the word 'tumour'. Is it cancer?" Claude continued without taking a breath. I guess, like me, she had had enough of Pedro's stalling.

There was a silence: all eyes were on Pedro as he took a deep breath, then answered, "It's a kind of, yes."

"So is it? You're saying the plasma cells is a cancer?" asked Claude, lips pierced and voice demanding.

"The plasma cells are a cancer, yes," he said, repeating Claude's exact words.

"So is that a confirmation?" Claude asked. The conversation now was sporadic, patchy and uncomfortable.

"Yeah, yeah, it is a confirmation," he replied, looking at his computer as if checking my notes.

"So did you get that from the test that Sharon took last week?" Claude spoon-fed, leaving no stone unturned.

"Yes, from the bone marrow, I just checked that," Pedro confirmed.

Danny and I looked at each other. Before anyone could say anything Pedro continued to explain the bone marrow process. Finally, he ended, saying the piece of bone that was taken proved that it is that kind of tumour.

"Right ok, that's what we wanted to know, so it's the plasma that causes the amyloid?" Claude confirmed, almost matter-of-factly, trying to keep it light for my sake.

"The amyloid is a kind of consequence of the cancer. Like if you had lung cancer, you can cough; the cough is a consequence of the lung cancer, in the same way the amyloid is a consequence of the tumour."

Somehow, although we knew the results, nothing prepared us for this confirmation. The already solemn mood suddenly dropped. We were so disheartened, my heart sank once more, and as if reading my thoughts, Jo consoled, "It is nothing that you've eaten; it's nothing that you've done. I don't know why this has happened; it's just one of those unfortunate things."

"Could I have done things better?" I asked, almost whispering.

"No, there's nothing you could have done," both Jo and Pedro responded in unison.

I consulted my list again and enquired about a booked flu jab I had prearranged for the next day. However, by talking it through, we all deduced that if the chemotherapy would kill off my white blood cells anyway, the flu jab would probably be a waste of time.

We continued to talk about diets and if there was anything I should or should not take to assist or obstruct the treatment.

Danny had interrupted, telling me that this kind of knowledge is more for the dietitians and I should not worry the doctors with supplements. I knew that Danny did not want the professionals interfering with his plans to take me down the alternative, holistic route.

"No, not really," piped up Pedro and Claude at the same time.

"It's quite relevant," continued Pedro.

Jo mentioned not taking St John's wort, as they specifically knew that it can interfere with the chemo and Pedro spoke about not having alcohol.

"What type of cancer is it?" I asked, a lump stuck in my throat with each breath I took. "What stage is it?"

Jo jumped in and explained that it was called multiple myeloma, totally different from breast cancer and other organ cancers. I was about to ask Jo what stage I was at, when almost intuitively she added, "Multiple myeloma cannot be measured in stages. Myeloma doesn't usually cause a lump, more often it affects the production of your good blood cells."

Claude continued to get clarity about multiple myeloma, any cures and the survival rate, which were not conclusive.

Jo touched on some of the symptoms. I certainly related to quite a few, especially the numbness and weakness in my legs and feet. I felt as if Pedro, Claude and Danny were giving me this 'moment' to talk to Jo. They remained silent as I systematically went through the few questions left on the list, all now totally directed at Jo, as she somehow seemed more knowledgeable around procedures and practices.

We left Pedro's office, Jo giving me a sincere and heartfelt smile, whilst confirming that we would see each other soon.

There was no need for us to discuss anything else, we finally got the confirmation, which deep down we knew all along. It had taken much longer to get there than anticipated. We never discussed it, but I am sure we'd all agreed that relaying test results is not Pedro's forte.

I could not look at either Danny or Claude, tears were welling up in my eyes, but I did not cry. Every negative thing that was spoken I silently disassociated myself with. As a Christian, I spiritually cut it off, that's all I knew to do. As we left the hospital, Claude also said, "Let's rebuke everything negative that has been said: we shall cut it off, in the name of Jesus." She then proceeded to mimic cutting things away from me, as we walked to the car. I realised then that, as I was walking into an unknown territory, my life would never be the same.

Chapter 9

OUR BILLY THE KID

Once home, I called our friend Bill (Billy the Kid, as Danny called him): he would know what to say, what to do. After all, it was now confirmed: I had the same cancer he had. I never heard the name myeloma before Bill was diagnosed, more than a year before, and I desperately needed to speak to him. There's definitely something in the saying, "who feels it, knows it". And he not only felt it, but also was certainly knowledgeable about the condition.

It was over a year since he had had stem cell treatment; and explained so meticulously that his bone marrow stem cells were removed and stored; he was then given a very high dose of chemotherapy to kill the abnormal, cancerous cells and then the stored stem cells were transplanted back. From what I understood, his procedure was done almost like a blood transfusion.

We had visited Bill in King's College Hospital just after his transplant and he had contracted an infection. He was so articulate and usually immaculate. When we walked in, we received the shock of our lives, we had not expected him to look like this, his typically smooth, handsome, light-skinned complexion was very dark; in fact, he was so black and patchy, I hardly recognised him. He had tubes everywhere, it was the ones attached to his nose and throat that looked most alarming. His usually glimmering eyes were dazed. Danny and I looked at each other in disbelief, then instantly tried to conceal our astonishment. He was frail and weak and could barely speak. My eyes watered and in typical Bill style, he motioned for me to come closer and whispered in my ear, "I'm fine, Shaz, it looks worse than it is." He was able to explain exactly what had happened.

The stem cell transplant had been a success; however, there were workmen in the hospital at the time and major construction work taking place on the ward. He had been left on a trolley in the corridor for a period of time, had used the toilet which everyone used. "Every man Jack," was how he put it; and subsequently, with his immune system low, contracted the infection.

I remember Danny and me praying for Bill there and then in the hospital and feeling great that he had received our prayers so openly. We saw him two weeks later, 'fit as a fiddle' when we paid him a visit at his sister's home.

Danny had turned to Bill, one of his best friends. 'My bona fide!' Danny liked to exclaim. I never heard him communicate with anyone the way he conversed with Bill. They seemed to know each other like brothers; the stories they knew about each other enabled them to tease each other in such a way that it was difficult to tell if they were serious or not. They had great conversations, with such laughter: we would all end up in tears. The minute I had met Bill we clicked in very much the same way Danny described how they had clicked all those many years before. In fact, I had become close friends with many of Danny's friends and family, especially his sister Lorna Gee and brother Martin. There was Raye, who was his best man's younger sister; from the day we were introduced, we became great friends. And his lifelong friend Cora (who subsequently was his nephew's mother-in-law) also became my trusted and loving friend, not to mention all his nieces and nephews, most of whom I adopted as my own. Danny always joked that all his friends and family adopted me, yet mine were much different with him. We finally concluded that he just had a lot more friends to go round.

Bill was tall, fair, very slim and, as my friend Angie would say, 'very pleasing on the eye'. We had a friendship which deepened the more we shared ailments and remedies, the knowledge of the pain of the bone marrow biopsies, the chemotherapy and all our tests and medication.

Danny had already warned Bill about what was happening with me, so my call came as no surprise to him. As I relayed exactly what Pedro had said, I knew he felt my anxiety. He said all the right words to encourage me, before slipping on his 'Dr Bill hat' and telling me what to eat, drink and what supplements to take, before, during and after the chemotherapy. "Cut out coffee, sugars and salt and drink plenty of water, at least two litres a day, from now on, especially during the treatment!" he encouraged. "And try and exercise where you can," he would continue, as he reeled off a list of supplements I should take.

He was an avid swimmer and runner, and ran and swam

many miles daily. I reminded him that I could just about get up a flight of stairs. To which he would say, "You can stretch and make sure you sit up instead of lying down when you can."

Unlike Bill's myeloma, which affected his kidneys, this myeloma (I refuse to claim it) affected my heart, and therefore stem cell or heart transplants were not options for me. I had read about the success rate of myeloma patients who had had either heart transplants, stem cell treatment, or both, and felt disappointed and quite saddened that I could have neither. The cardiologist had explained that I would not survive under that strain. A new heart would also be attacked by the abnormal proteins. Bill was so sympathetic when I explained this and said that we were all different and, as chemotherapy was my only option, it would definitely work for me.

Bill and I also discussed alternative options, like herbal remedies. He had weighed up the pros and cons and, coupled with his healthy lifestyle, deemed that chemotherapy would also work for him. Danny always said that if Bill had not been so fit and healthy before, he would never have made it through.

Danny was totally against me having chemotherapy. Once the word had filtered out to our friends about my condition, all and sundry came with books, recipes and cancer-curing tips, with anti-chemotherapy perceptions. It was no wonder he, too, became convinced that we should pursue alternative therapies and looked to the beliefs of Dr Sebi, a herbalist, verified and professed healer in Honolulu, who specialised in curing diseases. We went onto YouTube to listen to his teachings, which all sounded great. It was very encouraging, but as I said to Danny, it was too little, too late. I already had cancer and needed life-saving treatment. This was no time for me to suddenly start experimenting with 'eating healthily'. I would implement some of the foods and ideas, which were realistic; however, I was not convinced that all his practices, albeit great, could help me. For instance, I completely understood the concept of our bodies being acidic and, although the blood can be alkaline, there needs to be a balance. I had learnt all about balanced diets in school and had recently purchased a reduced Groupon course on diets and nutrition. I had learnt that to build up our bodies and maintain good health, it was important that we consume seven components of a balanced diet on a daily basis, with proteins being one of them. Dr Sebi begged to differ, saying proteins were not an essential part of your diet; in fact, he asked the question, "What is protein?"

Danny was pretty much converted: Dr Sebi had convinced him. I wasn't sure and needed to look into it some more; I just did not have that time.

Some of the things Dr Sebi said were thought-provoking and so true; like we had grown up piling up our dinner plates with rice and peas, a portion of meat and the tiniest portion of vegetables; when in reality it should have been piled up with vegetables, little or no meat and a little rice and peas. That I believed, but there were other things that I could not prove, which seemed to contradict those I had previously learnt.

Having been taught that our bodies needed amino acids, which were necessary to break down foods, essential to our bodies, and only produced from a balanced diet, I was now hearing that having an acidic body allows the growth of cancer cells (wasn't sure if it was the same acids), and in contrast cancer cells had no chance to grow in an alkaline body.

To stop the cancer cells I was advised to drink pure lemon juice, as it had the potential to make our bodies alkaline, thus preventing any cancer cells from growing.

Once the word had filtered out that I had cancer, most people went directly to Danny with their beliefs and opinions, the lemon/acid versus alkaline theory a very popular one.

I told Bill how Danny had gone out and bought me a bag of soursop leaves, cinnamon leaves, a packet of bicarbonate of soda pills, and twelve large, water-filled, fresh coconuts, as he had heard that they were all good at combating cancer in various ways and the coconut water was especially good for the heart and could lower blood pressure. Bill and I both laughed as I explained that I would be admitted to hospital in two days and my blood pressure was already too low!

Bill spoke in detail about having the transplant. He was very articulate and made me understand fully what he had just gone through. He explained that stem cells are mother cells, which have the potential to grow into any cell type in the body. He had hoped that as stem cells have the ability to self-renew or multiply, that it is just what they would do.

"Shaz, I'm confident that coupled with the chemotherapy, it would produce new cells and the process will work for me," Bill had said, trying to make me feel good.

Deep down, we both knew that nothing made the myeloma go away permanently: there was no cure. The stem cell transplant or chemotherapy isn't a cure for that type of cancer, and from what we learnt, the myeloma would often return.

Eight months later, Bill's Myeloma came back with a vengeance.

Bill explained that we all needed a balanced diet. He wanted me to stay healthy and even told me to write down 'milk thistle', so that when I had finished my chemotherapy I could take it to flush out all the chemotherapy residues left in my organs and system. He encouraged and influenced my physical healing so much. If he called whilst I was lying down, he would always say just sit up, if you can, it's better for your posture and condition. I felt his love at all times.

Chapter 10

HOSPITAL ADMISSION

Jess and I spent a few days organising my hospital bag, I was so grateful for her little Peugeot 106. Although she had only recently passed her test, she was persistently and willingly running to and fro, picking up last-minute toiletries, bedsocks, slippers, everything and anything she thought would make my stay comfortable. I had to remind her that she would have the opportunity to shop even after my admission.

We also set up a WhatsApp group, where we aimed to keep our large family and close friends simultaneously informed of the daily occurrences, treatment, medication and my well-being. There were over 50 members in the group, and it proved to be much more effective than any one of us could have ever imagined.

Soon we were sharing other things, congratulating family and friends who graduated, passed exams, celebrated birthdays, new jobs, holidays, everything. Prayers and words of encouragement flooded in and so the chat grew. We literally had our very own Facebook going on, just much more inspirational and rewarding. I made everyone aware that it was not just for me, and it worked wonderfully.

On the Saturday, Jess drove me to the hospital, we were to arrive by 2 pm. I was so proud of her. This was just weeks after her eighteenth birthday and she had grown into a beautiful, responsible young lady. I thought about her father, Phil; he would have been so proud of her, too: her own guardian angel, looking down on her and smiling at her achievements.

I recalled the night I was informed that he had died. His two sisters, Gina and Jo and their respective husbands, Paul and Mike, together with Phil's younger brother Peter came over about 1am. Waking me up, they gave me the bad news. I knew he was feeling ill the days before and we had assumed food poisoning; he hid the fact that, during the proceeding days, he had actually collapsed twice and was taken to hospital. Phil had a great fear of hospitals. As a child he had witnessed his mother's demise after she had spent lengthy periods in hospital, as well as witnessing his younger brother's death as a teenager. This irrational fear led him to discharge himself from A & E on both occasions, telling no one and vowing never to return. It was Jess's third birthday and we were supposed to take her out. He said he was feeling poorly, mentioned food poisoning, yet purposefully hid the extent of how terrible he really felt. Septicaemia had set in, from a perforated ulcer, this time when he had been rushed to hospital it was too late and he had no chance of survival. Yet when he failed to turn up for Jess's birthday party, I felt deep down that something bad had happened. I cried until the corners of my eyes were sore; they stung, and still I cried. Viv, Mum, Dad, and now Phil. How could this be? How would I bear this one? He was so young;

our children were still babies. I cried for him and everyone I knew who had died.

After the initial tears, the next thing I did was reach for the phone to call my mum. I knew she would know what to do, but as I struggled to dial her number, reality sank in: I had lost her two years before, and it was only just seven months since Papa G's death. There was no feeling of denial this time; I had been there with Mum and Dad, and I knew the exact finality of it all. I would never see him again. There was no use me sitting by the window; he was certainly not going to walk by.

I hugged our daughter Jess, just three years old; how would I ever explain to her that her father died on the day we should have celebrated her third birthday? I hugged her so tight, visualising that I was Phil, squeezing her so hard. She pulled away, I just wanted to hold her the way I'd seen him do so many times before. I recalled him hoisting her onto his shoulders, her squealing with delight, and then my screams for him to put her down and to be careful. How I would have done anything that day for him to do that again. Do it now, please do it now! Swing her around until she's sick. Everything I had told him not to do I was blaring at the top of my voice for him to come back and do. I wanted him to light a cigarette, invite his friends round, let them all smoke, smoke in the house, drive my car, and drive like a maniac. I wanted to give him the biggest plate of food, with a variety of stuff, just to watch him purposefully shuffle them around the plate with his fork, everything I had ever seen him do, good or bad, I just wanted to see him do it.

I always said he was the fuse in the 'enthusiasm' he portrayed to his children. And I felt that nowhere on this earth would anyone have that same passion or devotion for them.

As Jess drove me to St George's Hospital, my mind went straight back to those hours following his death. I had been driven to King's College Hospital. The long corridors of the hospital making the walk seem endless, I was taken to what seemed like a faraway, clandestine, candlelit chamber, with walls made up of velvet curtains, where his lifeless body lay on a bench, and a dark purple-coloured satin sheet was pulled up under his chin, I had stared in disbelief as I took the whole lot in. Despite everything, he looked peaceful and calm, as if he was asleep. I recalled touching his curly black hair, feeling his body, his cheeks, his legs under the satin sheets, they felt so stiff; in fact, his entire body felt so cold, firm and abnormal, my hands automatically went back to the only part of him that was unchanged, his curly hair. I wondered about the arguments we used to have. They seemed so trivial now, such meaningless things. Everything we ever argued about brought tears to my eyes, they were so mindless, insignificant and unimportant compared to life.

I met Phil at Granaries night club in Croydon, after our work's Christmas do. I was living in Valley Park, Croydon at the time and my cousin Ingrid and I wanted to polish off the night with some dancing. No recollection of how we stumbled on the club, as we had never heard of it before that night. Phil had a weekly spot there playing the piano and there and then he began serenading me, most of the night in the Piano bar. I thought he was so good looking; a little on the thin side, but quite the charmer. When I first met him, I thought, 'Is he for real?' He was such a practical joker and seldom took anything seriously: everything was a big joke and he loved to have a laugh. Then I met his family and from his wonderful father, Harold (God rest his soul), right down to all his siblings, they were all the same: very humorous and witty, with great stories to tell. There was always fits of laughter.

I kept hoping and thinking it was a sick joke and the cold body in front of me was going to disappear and Phil, the practical joker, would jump out from behind one of the purple velvet curtains.

The last thing I remembered at the hospital was hyperventilating; the Duty Sister brought me a brown paper bag and encouraged me to blow into it. I had never done that before; I felt light-headed but relaxed. I immediately tried to compose myself; the last thing I felt like being was dignified, yet I completely composed myself. Many years later, his sister Georgina, who had become a great friend, informed me that she was selfishly annoyed with my display of hyperventilation. She wanted me to stop, because I reminded her of the last days, as a teenager, she spent with her mother. I guessed seeing daggers from her would have been a good enough reason for me to be composed.

Once I returned home, all I knew was that I had to be strong for the children.

It was fifteen years on, and now Jess was without a doubt the one being strong for me. Staying with me at the hospital and telling me it would all be ok. She would not leave my side.

We were all silently concerned about Jess; she was studying her last year of 'A' levels, what they called A2, and would be sitting exams shortly. Her conditional offer at UCL to study medicine meant that she required A*s in Biology and Chemistry, and an A in Religious Studies; my illness could not have come at a worse time. Thankfully, I had a great family and friends support network, which was completely extended to my children, making them feel well supported.

Claude had been the one to contact my eldest son Josh, he hastily rushed down to the hospital, very concerned. I saw an overnight change in him, he had matured from boy to man in days, and we realised that, at 24, he was handling the situation extremely well. Josh had been a great child growing up, and a great teenager and student. He received impressive grades for his ten 'GCSEs' and three 'A' levels, giving him the opportunity to read Theology at Manchester University. It took him eighteen months before he realised it wasn't for him; at which point he applied to another 'Russell Group' university, Leeds. Successfully, he went through the full university entry process, and studied Media and Communication.

Unfortunately, this course lasted just over a year, due to what Josh claims was a spate of unfortunate incidents. He was 24 years old, working for a music college, for overseas students, when adamantly he signed up (third time lucky) for a three-year evening degree at Birkbeck University of London, to study Economics and Social Policies. So far, he hasn't looked back and overall he has never given me cause for concern. In fact, I was probably one of the last siblings to have my first child at age 27, which was certainly considered old by my family standards and practice. Prior to being a mum, my motto was: "Children should be seen and not heard". Whilst visiting friends and family, I never understood why offspring were allowed to be running throughout the house, jumping around and making noise, whilst parents ignored the fact, and if they needed them to do something, they would scream commands to them at the top of their voices. "Oh, sure, Sharon," a sister commented to me once. "If you had children they'd be sitting in a corner with glasses on, reading a book."

"That's right," I'd reply jokingly, whilst seriously thinking, 'Too right, he or she would.' And I suppose that's just what I tried to achieve when Josh was born. He was such a great child, well behaved and well mannered; he sat quietly reading on most occasions. It was no wonder he excelled at school.

I finally met Dr Willis, the haematology consultant, on the Sunday; she was such a considerate and refined lady. She was tall with short, blonde hair and very slim; a little dishevelled, but she certainly knew how to put herself together, when needed. Dr Jacky and Claude were with me when she came to see me. She confirmed treatment would start the next day. The monitoring of my heart had already begun. My whole torso was hooked up to the mobile heart machine. Dr Willis explained the treatment and how the three different doses would be administered; Velcade by injection into my tummy; five dexamethasone steroid tablets and seven cyclophosphamide tablets, which were toxic. She proceeded to inform us that, following the treatment, they would bring me a commode, as it was unlikely that 'my head would be able to leave the pillow'. My blood pressure was also extremely low, as a result of my failing heart, and this would have to be monitored closely.

Claude and Dr Jacky departed shortly afterwards, but not without praying that I would get through the treatment effortlessly. They also updated the WhatsApp group, which soon became known as the 'Family Group chat' and asked everyone of faith to pray for me also. My two sisters, Pat and Joan, in America were also part of the 'Group chat' and informed us that they and their respective churches were also praying for me. We had ministers and friends, as far north as Yorkshire and overseas, from Singapore to Jamaica, praying and extending their best wishes. We received daily well-wishes from practically everyone, sometimes prayers, words of comfort and exaltation, or just messages telling me they were thinking of me.

Chapter 11

STAND ON THE WORD

I had also been directed by my Pastor on how to receive my healing. "Stand on the word!" she had instructed. "Trust God and be sure to keep the faith!" Having purchased a book called *'90 Days to Possessing Your Healing' by Kynan Bridges:* I would read it daily and say the healing prayers which accompanied it.

Claude was angry that I was ill. It was clearly written in every breath she took. She fought hard to conceal her pain and anger, but it was impossible for her, who undoubtedly wore her heart on her sleeve. I knew she was crying and could not bear to think of losing another sister. She continually asked, "Why you, Shaz?" "What have you done to deserve this?"

One day, on my hospital bed, I looked up at her and said, "I'm reminded of a story in the Bible, John 9, where the disciples asked Jesus (and I'm paraphrasing) why a particular blind man was born blind; in fact, they asked him, 'Who sinned?' Was it the sin of his parents or himself? And Jesus had answered, 'Neither sinned, it's so that the works of my Father be made manifest in him.' Claude, likewise, I had replied, "I believe that this has happened to me and if I just have faith as small as a mustard seed, then God can heal me and HE will be glorified."

She took a deep breath. I saw her chest almost morph up into her shoulders; she said nothing, but was clearly distraught. Usually calm in nature, cheerful and content, she now seemed infuriated and short-tempered with everything and everyone around her.

Claude, although reluctant, would update the chat in line with my requests. If she had had her own way, she would not be updating anyone, or at least not so many people with what she deemed to be a private affair; she could easily have done without the WhatsApp chat. I, on the other hand, wanted to let all my friends and family know exactly how I was feeling and provide a daily account. (I often look back at the chat in great admiration.)

I also wanted everyone to pray every step of the way, as scriptures indicated that if one chased a thousand and two put 10,000 to flight, if we were more than two, and all stood together in agreement, then the magnitude of the prayers would be colossal. Everyone was updated with the treatment plans and meetings. What started out as my personal diary soon became a full-blown forum and blog.

Claude often told me that I couldn't afford to 'have anything against anyone'. I knew exactly what she meant, as physically and mentally I did not need to be affected or bogged down by any emotional heaviness. I explained to her that I felt so covered by prayer; as well as the friends and family that were praying for me, the day before my hospital admission, Pastor Denis and Lorna had visited me at home and prayed for me, I had also visited Pastor Curdell and she had asked me if there was anyone whom I needed to forgive, as unforgiveness could hinder my healing.

By the time I left the Pastor's house, where they had prayed for my healing and protection from the poison of the chemotherapy, I was ready spiritually, physically and mentally to receive the chemotherapy.

The night before the treatment my nephew, who was away in California, on business, called me. He said, "Auntie, I heard the treatment is starting tomorrow."

"Yes, Supe," I confirmed.

"Auntie, I need you to fight this with everything you have in you. This is a battle," he continued. "And you need to fight! Don't give in to this poison, Auntie, you can beat it. Auntie, do you understand?"

"Yes, Supe," I confirmed again.

"See you when I get back. I love you, Auntie." He was gone.

Supe was in his thirties, a very talented chemical engineer amongst other things; usually a man of very few words. I heard him. The fact that he had taken the trouble to call from so far away spoke volumes and mattered a great deal to me. I heard him with every fibre in my body. I would fight this poison physically, spiritually and mentally. The chemotherapy would do what it was supposed to, nothing more and nothing less. The battle had begun.

Chapter 12

THE FIRST CYCLE

The treatment nurses called at 8 am to say they would come up and administer the first dose of steroids shortly. They had popped in the night before to introduce themselves. Everyone spoke so kindly, they were very calm and considerate.

They explained that as one of the side effects from the steroid, the dexamethasone, was insomnia, they would come up first thing in the morning. They came with the phlebotomist, Peter, who visited me so many times to take my blood; eventually he became a friend. Peter was African, with a large frame; he always came with a song and a smile on his face. He really made me feel relaxed. All of the nurses and hospital staff wished me well, even the cleaners. They were all quizzical as to what my situation was and wondered what the outcome for me would be.

The doctors explained that after the treatment my immune system would be very low, as my white blood cells would be killed off, so as a precaution and to prevent any infection, I had my own room. It was on the first floor, overlooking A & E.

Having my own room was a privilege and a blessing, I could pray privately. I would have personal conversations with all who came in, which really distracted me from the reality of what I was going through and assisted with my mental healing.

I felt like Pollyanna: positivity bias, as someone once cited. In the midst of devastation, I had so much to be glad for. I knew the Lord and had faith that He would heal me, I had a supportive family, church and friends. Many had heard the bad news about me having cancer, they all came out of the woodwork in a great way.

When Danny and I had got married the year before, we had so many friends and family that we really could not do a traditional wedding, we did not want tables with nameplates or separating the evening guests from the morning guests. We did end up whittling the guest list down to 350 so that everyone could be invited for the whole day. We had poser tables, a BBQ and five food stations.

On the one hand, it was great having the restaurant, as we were able to drive down the cost, by doing the catering ourselves. However, on the other hand, it was to my detriment, as at 11 pm the day before, I was the one picking up last-minute utensils and equipment from the restaurant, dropping boxes off to the reception hall, swapping cars with my cousin Ingrid, picking up my stepdaughter Tianna from her home, while typically (and I'm not sure how much of this Claude knew) Danny was snuggly wrapped up in bed, from 9 o'clock, at his best man Ewart's home.

My wedding morning was not much better for me, as I ended up in tears. Having gone to bed at 2 am, I had to be up at 6 am, as my hairdresser, although brilliant, was unable to get to my house, so at the last minute all my bridesmaids' breakfast plans had to be abandoned. There was a lot of running around, on all our parts, to get our hair and make-up done. The photographer and videographer had turned up at the empty house to shoot the bridal party, in vain. The bridesmaids' car had broken down in Southampton and by the time I sat in the make-up chair at the MAC counter in House of Fraser; I was in floods of tears, crying uncontrollably. The make-up artist managed to calm me down. I am sure she must have done this a million times. "Get it all out now," she said, "because once I've finished your make-up there's no turning back."

To top it all, when I called Danny, he said he had slept well, woke up to a smoked salmon, champagne breakfast, lovingly cooked by Cee, Ewart's partner and a 'Leith' chef; the groomsmen had all arrived and their photographer was taking pictures. He was calm and more than ready to seal the deal. Our side was running around like headless chickens. My talented and creative cousin Ingrid was our wedding planner; she was also having a terrible start to the day; she went to oversee the hall decorations and my sister Juliet rushed away with her car keys, leaving her stranded at the hall and extremely late for our wedding. I found out after the ceremony that she had missed my entrance, which was such a shame, as she had assisted so much at the rehearsals. She had worked tirelessly, providing us with an excellent service from start to finish. We knew she would leave no stone unturned and she never took any money for her services. We had a cocktail theme, a BBQ, with five food stations, Caribbean, Chinese, vegetarian, fish and a delicious dessert station with a fruit tree as the centrepiece; everyone ate what he or she wanted, when they wanted, where they wanted. With so many guests it worked extremely well.

Juliet and my niece Kira, now in her twenties, taught us our wedding dance, they were brilliant choreographers, especially Kira. We danced to Natalie Cole's 'This Will Be (An Everlasting Love)'. We laughed so much, we had to cut it short, our unsuspecting guests, none the wiser, were so pleasantly surprised.

We knew many people, especially Danny, I always said. If he was walking in the deepest part of Africa, someone would pop up whom he knew. Even after knowing him for over nine years, his friends are so numerous, I struggle to remember who is who.

Everyone wanted to see me and show their support; I was inundated with messages from well-wishers. Eventually, Claude, my Rottweiler, was not allowing visitors, she was not taking any risks of me getting infections. She reduced the visitors to family only, and even then it was strictly monitored.

The first day of treatment, I waited all day for the chemo nurses to turn up. I was anxious; when they finally arrived, they explained that they were waiting for the blood results, as they could not administer the drugs without them. Once the blood results were in, checked and ok, they would then make up the drugs.

The dexamethasone was administered first, which was five small tablets, 10mg in total. Then a few hours later they arrived with the Velcade injection, as well as the cyclophosphamide, seven little tablets which were so toxic the nurses wore thick, purple gloves to dispense them and I was not permitted to touch them, so I almost threw them down my throat, from the small white cup, without touching my tongue.

The poison was in! Supe's words kept resounding in my head. "You have to fight this, Auntie." Now a waiting game. Dr Jacky and Jess had returned at 4 pm, to hold my hand. I was feeling fine. Later that evening, although bemused and groggy, I was a far cry from "Not being able to lift my head off the pillow", as Dr Willis had informed. I was out of bed, walking around, albeit slowly, but nothing like I was told.

A wonderful lady from a charity called Full Circle came and introduced herself to me: they provided free body massages to cancer patients and she booked me in for a foot and leg massage the following week.

Danny, Audrey and my children visited the first night and all seemed well. Danny was apologetic, as he didn't feel he was putting in the time with me, especially at this crucial time in my life. He had so much going on. Having to close and dissolve the bakery in Oxfordshire and trying to open a new restaurant in Herne Hill, near to Brockwell Park, within days of my admission, whilst dealing with my diagnosis, was no easy feat.

I released him as best I could. He knew I had a large support network and that afforded him the space he needed.

The fact that our previous restaurant had closed down a year before had a huge bearing on the success of this one. My family did not understand and thought I was being too lenient with Danny, but I knew from our previous experience what it took to get it off the ground. I remember saying that when the chef accidentally stabbed me in the elbow, the very first night we opened our previous restaurant, I should have known then what was in store for us, packed my bags, walked away from the restaurant business and never looked back. It certainly was an ordeal, although many great things came out of it. We had a brilliant turnout on the annual Brixton Splash days, where thousands visited the shop; the preparation, build-up and the climax were amazing. We had numerous celebrities who would visit us from far and near, whilst building up a great customer base, many of whom became our lifelong friends. We also built a fantastic brand.

During the night I was monitored very closely. The nurses came in every hour, for observation. In addition to the chemotherapy, I was taking other drugs, two and three times a day, from anti-nausea, antivirus, antacid, anti-fungi, sleeping pills, plus medication to assist constipation. The doctors were concerned about my blood pressure, which was very low, and my heart was registering abnormal beats on the monitor. From the readings, the nurses would often rush in to check that I was still alive. I felt the various heart palpitations, but on the whole and in the scheme of things, my body tolerated the chemo well and I was feeling fine.

The doctors carried out their rounds the following day; they were really impressed and surprised that I was actually able to walk around the room. The next day was basically the same as the first. Wednesday I was booked in and taken down by the porter for a tummy X-ray, as I was so constipated, still feeling fine, apart from a little tummy ache, but by the Thursday, the effects of the chemo started to set in, I was confused, exhausted, feeling nauseous, constipated and very lethargic. Although I explained that I felt a little confused, my body was pretty much worn out. Thursday was my worst day, then as soon as I started to feel myself again, it was time for the next dose. And so it went on, the next cycle was increased. Dr Jacky had timed it well so that she would be there when Dr Willis came to see me. She explained that as I was responding so well to the first dose, they would now "up the doses", and increase all the drugs by at least a third.

Before the second and subsequent weeks' dosages would be administered, my heart had to be fully examined by the heart failure team. Routinely Matt or Steve from Cardiology would come up and run all the tests to ensure that my heart would withstand the rigorous chemotherapy. Once they gave the go-ahead the Haematology Department would then check the blood, to make sure there was no infection, my immune system was not too low and the platelets were fine for me to continue with the next cycle. There was only one occasion, around the fourth cycle, where I had developed a chest infection and treatment had to be postponed.

By the end of the second cycle, I could see the effects of the steroid. I officially had 'steroid face', or 'moon face', as someone once mentioned: smooth-skinned, round and enlarged, with the cheeks and eyes quite puffy. My features had certainly changed.

Whilst having tests at the National Amyloid Centre, at the Royal Free Hospital, I recalled reading an article on the actor,

Michael York, where he had spoken about having amyloidosis and how he constantly had black rings around his eyes. I could certainly relate to this also, as I looked as if I had two big, black, panda-like eyes. The treatment was now taking its toll. Although my appetite was good, frequently hungry, I wanted to eat everything my family would bring in; however, my taste buds were not lining up with my brain; my tongue felt fat and I constantly had a bad taste in my mouth; most of the time I relied on memory to have any chance of enjoying what I was eating. I was suffering terrible insomnia, which lasted days upon end. I was fatigued, operating on 25% energy: it was no wonder I needed to be hospitalised all this time. My mind felt as if it was 'out of control', saying my head felt mushy was an understatement, and my brain frequently underwent periods of being disorientated and dazed.

I tried everything to get some sleep, listened to music, sermons, videos, nothing seemed to work until the doctors eventually prescribed zopiclone, the sleeping tablet. The annoying thing was, it worked well, but the nurses would wake me every four hours for obs., and I could never get back to sleep, it was a vicious cycle.

Chapter 13

THE AUDACITY TO BELIEVE

There weren't many people that I knew who had been hospitalised with cancer and left the hospital improved, either they had gone into a hospice, died in a hospital or home in a hospital bed. I was determined not to be one of those too familiar statistics. I wasn't ready to give up, and wanted to make a difference. Every day I read the Word of God and stood firm. Daily the WhatsApp group would send through various prayers on my behalf, and I believed that there was power in numbers. Every day I repeated, "One chases a thousand, two puts 10,000 to flight; we are more than two." I totally believed that I would be healed of this illness.

Trusting God for the last twenty years of my life and knowing that He had previously come through for me in so many ways before gave me the faith that I now needed to receive my healing. I had not grown up in a Christian home at all, far from it, in fact, our family home was undoubtedly far from God-fearing. A home of unsavoury language, smoking and heavy drinking, with the occasional party, where alcohol and food were casually sold. I remember in the 70s, (at party-time, when us children were tucked up in bed, or so they thought) a light in the kitchen being rigged up to a bell by the front door, so that if the police ever came, and they often did for noise pollution, whoever answered the door would ring the silent bell, so the kitchen would know to put away the money from the sale of curried goat and alcohol.

The only claim to Christianity in our home was my parents having been married in a Catholic church and christening every one of us.

I became a Christian in 1996, the year my sister Viv died and a year after she and Claude became Christians. I always remembered thinking, Christians haven't got a life, they must be so bored, or even crazy; it was no wonder that Claude was saved, God would definitely call her, if anyone. She was a homebody, such a 'goody two-shoes', everything was constant in her life. At almost 60, she has the same boss and lifelong friend, Annie, whom she has known since the age of fifteen, she also married the same man she had met as a teenager. In comparison, I was the total opposite, very happy-go-lucky, drank and smoked heavily, lived for today, partied hard and enjoyed life to the full, or so I thought. Claude had invited me to her church in Camberwell and, although I thought I was not ready to give up on my 'high society' living, an 'out-of-body' experience left me no choice.

My best friend at the time, Joan refused to accept my conversion. We had a great time growing up together, as teenagers it was exciting and provided some great memories. Her family were like my family, we were very close, I am Godmother to her first son and I was especially close to her two younger sisters Jackie and Anneth. Joan cried at the thought of me being baptised and said how saddened she was to lose me, her drinking partner and friend. There was no reassuring her. Although we lost touch for a few years, Anneth and I remained close friends and my love and relationship with their family has been constant throughout the decades.

Once I started to trust God and lean on Him, I grew wings, just like Dumbo and his 'not-so-magic' feather. I had the audacity to believe I could do anything.

One of my very first tests of faith was believing that, as a single parent, I could put not only one of my children through private schooling, but all three. Moreover, I did, having experienced all sorts of obstacles and barriers, I turned to praying and felt God move in my favour.

Through all adversity, issues and struggles, I learnt to believe the saying that peace was not the absence of controversy or adversity in my life, but the presence of God.

After three weeks of treatment, the doctors commented on how well I was doing and they were pleased with the way my body was tolerating the drugs. The haematologist explained that they would continue, at the increased doses with all the chemotherapy medications, to attack the disease more vigorously.

"How do you feel about this?" asked Doctor Willis one morning. I was so impressed at how they kept me informed every step of the way and made me feel that I was the major part of the decision-making process; even though this was all new territory to me.

The way the cardiology and haematology departments had been meticulously working together gave me great confidence; somehow I completely trusted them.

"Of course you've spoken to Dr Peters about this?" I asked.

"Yes, we weren't sure how the first dose would affect you, but you've tolerated the drugs really well and they will be monitoring you. It is important that we attack this tumour vigorously."

"Will the side effects intensify?" I asked. I was still experiencing insomnia, being kept awake mainly by the tingling in my fingers and toes, very constipated and yet hopeful that the laxatives would work.

"There is that risk, but you will be monitored very closely, every step of the way," she repeated.

"Ok. I'll be happy with that," I agreed. I was optimistic and thought that if it needed to be attacked then I would get through, tumour destroyed, sooner rather than later.

After the increased doses and the end of the first cycle, the medication was doing what it said on the tin; however, my heart became weaker and weaker. The monitor readings that were sent through daily were revealing progressive abnormalities in the rhythm of my heart, showing a rapid decline.

Chapter 14

CARDIAC ARREST... NO WAY!

It was Friday the 11th of December, at 10:30 am when Dr Peters came into my hospital room, alone. She asked if it was ok for her to sit down. I nodded and she sat on the chair nearest the door.

"So, Sharon," she began, "you're aware that we've had to come in a couple of times during the night to check on you." I wasn't sure if it was a question or a statement, my mind was totally cloudy that morning, so I didn't respond, I just smiled, corners of my mouth quivering.

"That's because," she continued, "your heart has often been registering as if it has stopped. Have you been feeling palpitations or tremors?"

"Yes sometimes, but it just feels like slight palpitations. I haven't been worried because I'm taking comfort knowing that I'm connected to the monitor," I answered.

"Well, it's more serious than just palpitations, your heart is almost crescendoing to a point of arrest." I had read about the various heart failure stages and knew that I was in between stages 2 and 3 in heart failure terms, which relatively meant at worst I experienced palpitations and shortness of breath, and I was unable to do regular tasks. I was also aware that there was no turning back from stage 2 to stage 1, with no expectation that the functionality of my heart would improve. Medication would assist and/or God could heal my heart.

"What does that mean?" I asked, completely unprepared for her response.

"Sharon, your heart is at risk of cardiac arrest; I need to inform you that your life expectancy will be six months. There's nothing that can be done now."

I was silent. My eyes welled up with tears and they started falling down my cheeks. This was unexpected and I was in shock. I felt as if I was in front of a judge who had just sentenced me to death by lethal injection.

"Is there anyone you'd like me to call?" she said quickly, as if shocked by my response. But how was I supposed to react? I never expected this: 'six months'. My brain was going ten to the dozen, and my eyes were flickering as I attempted to stop the unexpected tears; there was no stopping them. My six month mental calculations took me straight forward to the 11th June 2016 and it was hard to get that date out of my mind. She repeated the question.

"No, no one," I answered, quickly this time.

"I think we ought to let other members of your family know," she retorted. "It's not a good idea to bear this alone."

"Ok," I responded, whilst thinking it was apparently alright for you to tell me whilst I was alone. You having second thoughts now?

"I'll tell my husband," I said. She could see the disturbance and confusion on my face.

"Would you like me to speak to him? I think it would be best if I met with your husband and informed him myself."

"Yes ok, then," I answered, now quietly sobbing. She patted me on my shoulder and left just as quickly as she had come in.

Chapter 15

MY LIFE FLASHED BEFORE ME

It all seemed so surreal, I was in a daze. My mind went straight back to the day when ruthless thieves robbed our payroll department whilst holding a sawn-off shotgun to my head.

Why my mind went back there, some 30 plus years before, I do not know. The words, 'Trauma! Trauma!' kept going around in my head. I was only nineteen years old at the time, yet I recalled every moment of it as if it were yesterday.

I was working as an accounts clerk, in Peckham, South-East London, for Evan Cook, a removal and shipping company, which was part of a large international shipping group called the Wingate Company.

I had left school in February 1982 at eighteen, the careers officer found me a job whilst halfway through studying my 'A' levels, for Pure and Applied Maths and Physics. I often wonder why I was taken out of school in the midst of my studies when I thought I was doing so well. I was sorry we did not know better at the time; however later in life one of my friends put it down to: unconscious bias', All I saw was pound signs, as here I was working for a fantastic company, earning my first real wage. Working with a wonderful boss Gerry, who believed in me and taught me everything he knew about bookkeeping and payroll, even sending me for evening classes to study for a AAT degree.

Every Thursday, as soon as the security firm, Group 4, delivered the cash, Ann, our wages manager, as she was known back then, would call me into her office to assist her with filling the 200 or so little brown paper envelopes. Group 4 would deliver the cash specifically broken down for us, from denominations, which we had sent to them a few days before. This was supposed to be like any other Thursday, but it wasn't. We bolted ourselves into her tiny office and sat down to count the money for all the warehousemen and their foremen. I enjoyed counting lots of money and putting it into the envelopes; it made the day go really fast. We were only ten minutes into counting when, my boss, Gerry knocked on the door. (Although unusual for us to be interrupted, we didn't think anything strange about it at all.)

"Who is it?" Ann asked as she continued to count the money.

"It's Gerry, open the door!" came the reply. I instinctively stood up and walked to the door, automatically lifting the large, wooden bar that reinforced the lock. As I turned the key, barely turning the handle, the door burst open with great force, pushing me to the floor. My stomach did a few somersaults as I hit the floor, screaming.

The thieves had tricked their way into our section of the building which dealt purely with finance, tied up the six other office staff, and threatened to shoot my boss with the sawn-off shotgun, if he didn't get us to open the door. I sat on the floor screaming, looking up the barrel of a gun and being screamed at to shut up. (I later learnt it was a double-barrelled sawn-off shotgun.) We were callously robbed of all the cash, yet I didn't see anything, I understood afterwards that I went into complete shock. After the robbers had left, everyone could describe what their appearance was, how their helmets had covered their balaclavas, which obscured their faces; how one had walked over to the desk and cut the phone line; what type of bag they had bundled the cash into. The whole episode was relayed by all, except me, in great detail.

Apart from the barrel of a gun, I saw nothing. I had never heard of a sawn-off shotgun; nor had I ever seen one. No one was physically hurt, but I always said that mental damage was far worse because no one can see the true harm. I couldn't go back to the office at first. Every time I went to work, I had panic attacks, as I believed the thieves were coming back. I kept repeating, "They have seen my face, they know who I am." It was even necessary for me to visit my GP, where on one occasion I was so distressed that I asked her for a cigarette. We both ended up smoking in her office, and in the midst of the small, smoky room, I cried my eyes out, as I relayed the fear and anxiety I was feeling after the robbery. I departed her surgery to the waiting room, where I quickly linked arms with my waiting sister Juliet and left walking suspiciously down the road, looking around as if I was being followed.

I was on medication and remember spending many days alone in my room, just sitting in the dark. At the time, I was affected so badly, and as I recall this story, which took place over 30 years ago, it still feels as if it was yesterday. Sometimes I find it difficult remembering what happened hours ago (especially with what we call 'chemo brain'), yet this episode of my life, I remember it too well.

They ended up finding one of the culprits, who had gone on to do another job and the fingerprints matched the fingerprints on the tape that he had left behind when they taped everyone up. He was sentenced to nine years and the worst thing was, I found out, years later, through a subpoena which revealed his real name, that he actually knew me and had frequently spoken to me in the off-licence across the road from the office. I am not sure what affected me more.

I thought about that near-life-and-death situation, where a gun was held to my head. One of the many traumatic situations in my life.

As I now lay slumped on the cold, hospital floor, I curled up in a foetal position and sobbed my heart out. Wow! This was totally unexpected; I knew that if I hadn't made it to the consultant when I did, I would not have made it through, but not now, not after the big scare, the start of treatment, I was not ready to throw the towel in just yet. All I could think about was my children. What would they do without me? Between the news, medication and the tears, I didn't know where I was. I was so distraught. This new update was enough to send my weak heart into arrest; if the heart monitor measured grief, I would be dead. Jo, my Macmillan nurse, walked in, not sure if she was sent in or if it was coincidental; she literally scooped me up from the floor and guided me onto the bed. She held me in her arms and allowed me to cry, whilst quietly repeating, "I know, I know." She held me softly and close to her until I fell asleep.

Awaken by Danny, he said he had received a call from Dr Peters and he had just come back from a meeting with her.

"I hate that doctor," he said, slamming the door. "She has no clue what she's saying, she has no right to say such things," he was clearly angry by what he had just heard. But what he said next completely shocked and pleasantly surprised me. "I told her straight, we do not accept that. We believe in God; our trust is in Him. I can't stand her."

"Dan, she's just doing her job, she's ok; I think you're being a bit harsh." As we hugged each other, I was quite proud of him, he refused to believe or accept what she had said. Yet my usual 'mustard seed faith' was diminished. How would I receive my healing if I did not believe? Somewhere deep down I knew that my healing begins in my spirit, just as I had received salvation by faith. I knew I had to receive my healing in the same way. Danny was showing faith that I had never seen in him before.

He was holding me tight and sighing deeply. My mind went back to the day before I was admitted to the hospital. Maybe that experience had lifted up something strong within him.

That day, when Danny and I had visited Pastor Curdell, for ministry, at her invitation, on arrival she took me upstairs to her prayer room (leaving Danny downstairs in her study, browsing through her books). Barely able to ascend her stairs, I crawled up slowly. Pastor Curdell prayed a very long prayer, quoting many Biblical scriptures (Hebrews 11:1 and Romans 10:9 stood out). She prayed about forgiveness and expressed how important it was for me to forgive anyone who had hurt me.

"It doesn't matter how small, make sure you do not hold anything against anyone," she reiterated, "and remember Matthew 6, the Lord's Prayer says, and forgive us our debts, as we forgive our debtors. Your healing begins in your spirit. Your confession brings possession. Do you understand?" she asked firmly, voice raised. She continued to pray against the effects of the cancer and the chemotherapy.

"As far as I'm concerned, cancer comes with a spirit of death, and I cast out the spirit of death from your life," she commanded in prayer, taking authority. Pastor and I spoke about anyone whom I may not have forgiven, I forgave them and asked God to also forgive me. Prayer done.

I came down those stairs much better and stronger than I had ascended. Even Danny commented that something had certainly changed spiritually.

Now here was Danny, being strong and with faith, consoling me, when usually it was the other way around. Whispering in his ear, I said, "Dan, this is between you and me, I don't want the children or anyone else to know what Dr Peters has said. In fact, I really do not want to see anyone today; let everyone, including the children, know that I'm extremely tired and do not want any visitors for the rest of the day."

He agreed. "We won't disclose what she had said, we will keep it a secret, as no one else needs to know."

Chapter 16

MUSTARD SEED FAITH

The next morning, the 12th of December, was the day of the restaurant launch. I was unsure how Danny would have got through the day, but I knew he would certainly be directing any negative energy into making the day a success. I, on the other hand, was feeling faithless and diminished. I decided to call Pastor Curdell.

"Hi, Pastor."

"Sharon!" she said livelily, clearly glad to hear my voice. "How are you?"

"Pastor, my faith level has dropped, I haven't got 'mustard seed' faith. I need your help, Pastor."

"Sharon, you can do all things through Christ who strengthens you." She started with the scriptures and continued to quote a few others. Hastily, she interrupted herself, as if suddenly realising where I was. Then in order to ascertain how best to direct me, she asked, "Are you lying down?"

"Yes, I am."

"Sharon, put your phone on the pillow." She then proceeded to reel off more scriptures and then she started singing to me in the most angelic voice.

"Be still for the presence of the Lord, the Holy One is here..." She sang all the verses and then she must have quickly looked it up and found it on YouTube and played it over and over again. For someone in their late-seventies, Pastor had certainly kept up to date with technology, and had all the latest apps. She had previously shown me how to upload and purchase books, on a 'Kindle app,' as well as the best video downloaders. Now here she was singing and playing the sweetest song down the phone. I was crying, but this time tears of adoration for what God was doing and a sense of release. I was shocked. My usually quite reserved Pastor was singing to me, down the phone. It was beautiful, timely and so soothing. She left me with the scripture about having faith as big as a mustard seed: from Matthew 13:31–32. I felt invigorated and comforted. A peace came over me, which was powerful enough to restore that which had disappeared when Dr Peters walked out of my room the previous day. I was uplifted. Pastor Curdell said we would 'cut off' everything that the doctor had said. She would send me the song for me to meditate on, said goodbye and hung up. Her job done. That day I had eleven visitors: Zack and his girlfriend, my sisters Polly, Audrey and her husband Winston, Jess, Auntie Dorrett and her husband Errol, Dr Jacky, Supe and Claude.

Everyone knew it was the launch day of the shop and they all had the same assumption that most people would have gone to support Danny and I would not have any visitors. That day, with my mustard seed faith, in the midst of knowing what Dr Peters had said, I welcomed my guests, who were all oblivious to what had been said, and had a fantastic day.

The launch had been a great success, over 200 people attended the restaurant and everything had gone to plan. Danny was exhausted. We had spoken over the phone and, although I knew he would have much rather stayed at home on the Sunday, he still turned up, albeit very late. "You were so missed, babes," was the first thing he said as he gave me a kiss and slumped on the bed, almost disconnecting the green wire to the heart machine as he lay down beside me.

"You know everyone sends their love and best wishes, don't you?" he asked as he patted my leg. He was very thrilled about the turnout and the support he had and rambled on in excitement for a good half-hour, telling me about the dishes, recipes, customers and the great responses, before he asked how I was feeling.

"I'm tired," I said, wearily, whilst thinking I had said enough. I could see he was exhausted and had already switched off. He ended up borrowing a pair of pyjamas and sleeping in the chair all night, until late afternoon.

Chapter 17

THE VEST OR ICD IMPLANT?

I had three weeks of treatment, then one week off. It was now just over four weeks since admission and I was experiencing the hardest week since the start of the medication. I felt as though I was functioning with less than 10% of energy. I was unable to sit up, even to read, all I could do was lie down. I felt as if the medication was really taking its toll on my brain and my body.

Whilst Danny was still at the hospital, Dr Peters came to visit us again; she examined my chest and back with her stethoscope; then, nodding her head, informed us that there had been some developments and it would be a good idea to call members of my family for a meeting.

"What developments?" I enquired, my voice quite brash and much louder than I had intended.

"I think you can talk to us two now," said Danny, equally abrupt. She looked at me for my approval. I nodded my head and she said, "Ok." She did not attempt to sit down this time, but looking at me, she walked to the end of my bed, picked up my notes, then began. "Now you both know the issues we spoke about with your heart. The results of the monitoring have revealed that your heart is at serious risk of cardiac arrest." Before we could ask what that meant, she continued. "This means, and I'll try and explain it as clearly as I can." She paused as if trying to convert her words into 'layman's terms'. "Ok, so the lower chambers of your heart, the ventricles, are not pumping the blood correctly. The palpitations you feel are when the heart is possibly quivering instead of doing its job properly, going into a dangerous rhythm; this can stop the heart beating suddenly." She paused as if waiting for either of us to ask a question. We didn't. We were both too eager for her to get to the point. She therefore continued. "Now, we cannot give you beta blockers to regulate your heart, as they are not compatible with one of your current meds, the medication you are taking to prevent infections, and quite frankly, beta blockers may not be sufficient in your case, if you are to leave the hospital."

"What do you mean if I leave the hospital, Doctor? What are you saying?" I enquired, puzzled by all she had said. She completely ignored my question, then responded in robotic fashion. "That leads me to the next point... There's something called a defibrillator. Have you heard of this?"

"Yes, isn't that what ambulance men use to shock you when your heart stops? I've seen it many times, even on the programme *Casualty*."

"Yes, that's what a defibrillator does. But there are various kinds and we believe that you cannot leave the hospital unless you have one." Well, if Pedro went around the bush when hesitating to say I had 'cancer', Dr Peters was his total opposite. I was lost.

"Will I have to carry a defibrillator all the time?"

I recalled working at a psychiatric hospital, where the health and safety manager had insisted that we purchased one and I had organised the relevant staff training. Although I had never used one, I noticed it was stored in a rather large briefcase.

"There are two types that we would like you to look at. One is a vest that you wear at all times and the other an implanted device," she said, interrupting my thoughts. Then continued. "If you'd like more information, I'll make an appointment with Janice, the Head of Pacing, to come and talk with you." Dr Peters' expression remained very flat. I really liked her, but I still could not comprehend what she was actually saying.

"What would you recommend, Doctor?" asked Danny casually, as if it made no difference what she proposed.

"Well, we've assessed your situation and we all believe that your risk of arrest is so great you would need something put in place before leaving the hospital. My advice would be the implant, but if you're against that, perhaps we can consider the vest."

Ok, so there are various defibrillators; I then pictured something like a bulletproof vest, which sounded impractical, but I didn't like the sound of anything implanted. After all, I was trusting that my heart would be healed. The medication was working well. According to Dr Willis, the protein light chains (how they measured the myeloma cells) had gone down quicker and better than what they had expected. There was an urgency in Dr Peters' voice. Both Danny and I sensed it strongly, and trying to sound rational, I said, "I'd like to hear more from the Head of Devices and speak to the family." This came out as if our family were the 'Mafia'. "Janice in Pacing," she corrected. "Ok, I will call you once I've spoken to her. I will also make an appointment for myself and Dr Willis to meet with select members of your family."

Janice from Pacing came later that afternoon. There was no appointment and Danny had already left. Janice was short and plump, probably late-fifties, well dressed and attractive with mousy-brown, short hair; she burst into my room like a bull in a china shop. She was pitching the option of the implanted cardioverter defibrillator, which she referred to almost lovingly as the ICD. Janice had brought with her a sample device, which she passed to me, saying, "See, this is exactly what we would implant, it would be implanted here," as she patted the upper part of her left chest.

"Just below the collarbone, under the skin. There will be a couple of wires connected to the device and attached to the valves of your heart, through the veins." Her tone was edgy, as if she had already run out of patience. She rattled off the details automatically, as if this was the tenth time she had described the procedure for the day. I was not going to be bullied into having this implanted device. I looked at the device; it was almost heart-shaped, made of hard, shiny metal and was about 6 centimetres long, 5 wide and a centimetre thick. It felt a bit heavy to me. Scornfully, I immediately handed it back. She explained that the device resembled a pacemaker, preformed the same job and more. It had the added capacity to record everything that occurred with my heart, as well as being able to shock it back into starting again, should it ever stop. I would have a machine connected at home, which would provide the hospital with readings and alert them to anything inappropriate that may be going on with the heart.

I stopped listening halfway through, I knew Danny was dead against any implant and I had decided I was definitely not putting my body through the stress of having an operation to implant any devices and I certainly was not keen on her seemingly hard sales tactics. I asked her about the vest option.

"Oh that's not my department," she said dismissively. "My understanding is it would not be feasible in your case anyway."

"Ok," I said. I had heard enough from Janice. She left the room as abruptly as she had arrived. I felt she was not impressed with my detachment from 'her baby'. She left behind the sample device, with a pamphlet; another sales tactic, I thought.

A meeting was set up with my family and the doctors, in my room for Wednesday the 14th of December, at 7 pm. Both Dr Willis and Dr Peters attended. Danny, Dr Jacky, Claude, her children, Supe and Michelle, also joined us. As I sat up straight in the bed, Claude and Danny sat either side. Everyone else remained standing.

Claude started by introducing herself and all the members of the family and their vocations. She emphasised both Dr Jacky and Michelle's medical experience. Dr Willis began saying, "Sharon, so far we have been extremely pleased with how your body has been tolerating the drugs and how well the myeloma has reacted to the chemotherapy. Remember I had said you would probably not get your head off the pillow, well, you have certainly proved us wrong in that respect. Haven't you?" I smiled at her. I was actually very fond of Dr Willis; she was so unassuming and caring and had a real flair about her. I was also very impressed at the way both departments worked so well together. I remember pointing this out to Jo once and in response she whispered knowingly, "Women head both departments, that's why."

Dr Willis walked over to me, sat on a chair by the bed and sympathetically articulated in a low voice, "If it were down to the treatment alone, you would be fine to leave the hospital now and receive treatment as an outpatient. We are very confident that the treatment is working as planned." Everyone nodded his or her agreement as she continued.

"We have been speaking with Dr Peters and the cardiology team and as you know there are concerns with your heart."

"Dr Peters," she beckoned, as she gave her the floor, whilst pointing to her, palm up. Dr Peters addressed me, voice sombre but firm. "Have you had a chance to discuss with the family our concerns?"

"Yes, of course," I said. "We've discussed your ideas surrounding the defibrillators, we all wanted to get more information, to weigh up the pros and cons."

"That's good," she said, looking around and directing her question at the various family members.

"So do we all understand why we have suggested that Sharon has a defibrillator?" Some of us responded, saying, "Yes." Claude came straight in, her attention towards Dr Peters and looking her square in the face.

"If the treatment is working, why can't we assume that Sharon's heart will make a full recovery?" I could see Dr Peters choosing her words well, as she was mindful that not everyone was aware of the six-month death sentence she had previously pronounced on me. After a long pause, she replied, "Even if the myeloma is cured today, well, we would call it 'going into remission', the heart has already been damaged and the functionality impaired, it's just not working in a trustworthy way." After another short pause she continued.

"And the blood show that, even though the chemotherapy is working, the myeloma is still evidently there. Potentially with the risk of increased damage to the heart."

"Ideally, Sharon, we would like you to be discharged in time for Christmas and have you home with your family, only attending the day unit for treatment, as an outpatient." Dr Willis interjected.

"However, with the continued treatment, the heart would be under pressure from the chemo as well as the already present amyloid," Dr Peters continued, almost ignoring Dr Willis.

"How many more cycles of chemotherapy does Sharon require?" asked Dr Jacky. I could see her mind going somewhere else.

"The current plan is for Sharon to have eight cycles of chemo," answered Dr Willis. "She's just completed the first cycle, so seven more to go. Which should take us up to, let me think, August, September time 2016?" Hmm, I thought to myself, if Dr Peters' prognosis were right, I would be long gone by then. I gulped at the thought.

"And if the chemo continues to work, surely the risk on her heart would be lessened?" Dr Jacky half-enquired, but stated strongly.

"Yes, that's the plan, but we can't take the risk in the meantime. Quite frankly, I'm not happy for Sharon to leave the hospital without a defibrillator, especially as the tests show that the heart is weakened and the lining quite stiff. Heart failure is certainly threatened," answered Dr Peters, putting it bluntly.

As the conversations progressed, the situation was clear; it was no longer a case of why I needed a defibrillator, it was which one. Vest or implant? We had looked at the various vests online during the day, and I started to warm to the idea, until Supe asked a very good question.

"How long would Sharon keep the vest on during the day and on what occasions would she need to remove it?"

Dr Peters responded. "Well, she would have to remove it each time she showered or bathed, and if she went swimming, those would be the key points."

"So," said Supe, "the chances of Sharon having a heart attack whilst not wearing the vest are very high, especially as we know that lots of heart attacks occur in the bath." Supe was a man of very few words, highly intellectual, but when he spoke, it was with purpose and often made good sense.

"Yes, that's one of the main advantages of the ICD. You have an added security at all times."

"Yes, but if you compare the two devices, I can't imagine there being any side effects with the vests, yet I would guess quite a few with the implant," said Claude sceptically, as she rubbed my leg and looked at Michelle for confirmation.

"They both come with pros and cons, Mum. With the vest, I've heard of it going off prematurely and also burning someone's skin when the liquid oozed out," Michelle added, "Nonetheless, I would agree there must be a lot more side effects with the implant. What might they be, Dr Peters?"

Dr Peters referred to her list. "With the ICD there's always a risk with any operation, whether it's bleeding on incision or insertion; there is the risk of infection, bleeding around the heart, what we call 'effusion'. The lung can get punctured due to trapped air, or damage to blood vessels or nerves near the device." Claude picked up my notebook and pen and started writing down the side effects.

"How common are these side effects and could the defibrillator go off inappropriately?" she asked.

"All these side effects are quite rare," responded Dr Peters. "The main point is for the defibrillator to work when it's needed, to shock the heart should it stop; which in Sharon's case is quite likely."

"Do you know what percentage of patients get the side effects and which ones are more common?" asked Dr Jacky. The two doctors both seemed to be working it out in their heads until Dr Peters said, "The side effects present differently in all patients. I'm not sure at this moment: I have not seen many myself. However, I can look this up and if this were the route that Sharon wanted to take, I'm sure I could get some figures to you. I recently had one patient who developed an infection and had to have the device removed, but that happened within days and did not cause any lasting issues."

"How often could it go off and would it need to be fixed each time?" I asked, suddenly my voice croaky again.

"You would be required to attend the emergency department if and when it went off and the device would be checked and reset," answered Dr Peters, looking directly at me.

"How long would Sharon need the device in?" Danny piped up in a low and controlled voice. He still would not look at Dr Peters who replied gravely, "Sadly it would be implanted for years."

"Years?" questioned Claude and Danny simultaneously.

"How many?" asked Danny, displaying the shock that we all felt.

"They can be implanted for up to eight years, sometimes more. I believe the battery life is quite long. They are checked a few times a year and tend to work consistently."

"So it has a battery: can this leak, then?" asked Supe.

"I believe that may be one of the side effects," Dr Peters acknowledged nodding in confirmation.

Everyone seemed shocked, especially surrounding the life of the device; this was certainly new territory to me and I was learning something very different and difficult to take in. In the midst of all that was going on and the heaviness I was starting to feel, I looked around the room with great pride. It was good to have such a balance of professionals around me: each came with their own expertise, asking quality questions, so significant and of great importance, and this meant so much to me. I wondered how difficult it would have been if I had no one, yet I felt as if I had the best team, the 'A' team. I knew I had a 'B' team and right down to a 'Z' team if needed. I was so fortunate. I felt God's love and provision right there in the room, even under the circumstances, knowing I was so unwell.

"Look," said Dr Peters, "we've certainly given you a great deal to think about. Time is not on our side, so please contemplate and consider all that has been said today. Any questions, please call us. Sharon, you have my direct number, don't you?" I nodded, as she continued. "We would need your response by the end of the day, whatever you decide." Both doctors said their goodbyes and promptly left.

We had all the facts, we had to make a decision, and the doctors had left us to it.

Chapter 18

THE BIG DEBATE

Supe started the debate. "The ICD seemed the least favourable option, but now I don't believe the vest is a secure enough alternative, especially if you have to take it off every day." He spoke about the likelihood of me not having it on at crucial times and threw out some percentages and statistics, which went straight over my head, but everyone seemed to agree and, to be honest, they said it made a lot of sense. We discussed the type of people and illnesses where individuals would benefit from having a vest, but it soon became clear that it posed too big a risk in my situation.

"I was totally against the implant to begin with, but I'm figuring that it may be the only option for you, Auntie," Supe said as he looked around for the others' opinions. Dr Jacky was online looking up data and researching the risks and side effects, whilst we all deliberated and conversed about the pros and cons. Michelle agreed with Supe and said, "I guess there are risks to everything, but without the defibrillator implanted, Auntie, you will be at more of a risk." Dr Jacky came back into the discussion, reiterating the side effects, but also agreeing with Michelle's point; there were so many points. After at least

40 minutes Claude said, "As much as it grieves me to see you go through any more pain, I think the implant would be the best option for Sharon. Shall we have a vote? Who thinks we should go for the implant?" Everyone put his or her hand up except Danny and I. It wasn't as if I was unsure. I was certainly of the opinion that I had no option: I wanted to see what everyone else thought.

"Danny, what's your take?" asked Claude.

"We didn't ask about infection, especially with Sharon's low blood count; surely that would be a big risk," he answered softly.

"I think that's covered, Dan," said Dr Jacky. "Sharon is presently on a lot of medication to counteract infection, and I'm sure they would not operate if there was too much of a risk."

"Is it really tried and tested, though? Sometimes these doctors just love to cut people open." I could see Danny was speaking from all the hurt he was feeling. He was not really weighing things up as well as everyone else.

"Dan, please, they know what they are doing. I really trust this team. I think it's for the best," I said, pleading with him to understand. A word popped in my head, 'Antidisestablishmentarianism', one of the longest words I had ever heard: my children had taught me it when they were in primary school. I knew it had nothing to do with doctors, but meant opposition to the Anglican Church in politics and religion. And true enough, as we sat there debating that word came to me: it felt like a word I could relate to Danny, with his feelings about the doctors and the pharmaceutical companies, Danny and his conspiracy theories. He knew he had to come around and after a few more repeated questions, which were directed mainly at Dr Jacky and Michelle, he seemed to be more accepting.

We had decided to go ahead with the implant. I was in disbelief. Last week I had never heard of the device, let alone intended to have it implanted in me.

Danny called Dr Peters, who seemed pleased with our decision. "I really believe it's for the best," she told him, "and please let Sharon know I'll be in to see her before the end of my shift," she announced as he hung up the phone.

By the end of that day, I had Dr Peters, a surgeon and Pedro all visit me with information about the imminent operation. Once we had told them that I would go ahead with the implant, it was full steam ahead and the date was set for Friday the 18th of December 2015.

Chapter 19

THE OPERATION

I was required to have a minimum of twelve hours of fasting before the operation.

"Now remember, no food after 12 midnight," Laura, my favourite nurse had warned me. "The procedure will take place whilst you are heavily sedated, under local anaesthetic," she continued.

"Why not general?" I interrupted. "Surely it's quite a critical operation." Laura sat on the bed, looked me in the eye and soothingly explained. "As a rule, it's normal to only have a local. It can be under a general anaesthetic if you want. However, with less than a week before Christmas, the recovery time under the general could take much longer, sometimes up to five days. The doctors want you out before Christmas and I'm sure you'd agree with them, eh?" She smiled gently as she patted my hand. Although I would have preferred to be totally knocked out under the general anaesthetic, I guessed it made sense to provide me with a better chance of being out by Christmas, especially whilst all the professionals purposed to discharge me so I could spend what they deemed was my last Christmas with my family.

Laura sat with me for a while. We had grown familiar over the six weeks since my admission. I would give all the nurses my chocolates and Laura was the only one who refused. She would smile the most beautiful smile and jokingly she would say, "You're the one having chemotherapy, you need as many chocolates as you can get." She was Irish, early thirties, tall, blonde and gorgeous, with her hair neatly spun up in a bun and held in place with numerous clips. She spent many an evening sitting in my room, asking about my children and telling me about her family back home in Dublin. She was travelling on the day before Christmas Eve to spend the holidays with her parents and younger sister.

"Hopefully you will be home before I leave for Ireland on Wednesday," she nodded and smiled as she spoke, her kindness coming through in her voice. "Don't know about you, but I can't wait," she continued excitedly.

"Hmm," was all that mustered out of my mouth with the tears. I didn't need to say any more; Laura understood, handed me a tissue and gently rubbed my shoulder. For the first time for as long as I could remember, it just did not seem like Christmas to me. Christmas for me was never last-minute: I would shop for weeks for the children, Danny and family. I would order the turkey in advance, usually from Mark's, a duck from Soho and all the trimmings would be stored up.

I had been in hospital for almost six weeks and, although the nurses did all they could to make the wards feel festive, I had arrived mid-November and the weeks had flown by in a whirlwind. I certainly wasn't at all prepared and this Christmas seemed alien to me. If I was discharged in time, Claude had insisted that we were all coming to her and she would prepare everything. As if reading my mind, Laura piped up. "Your sister said you're all going to her this year, that will be lovely, so let's wipe them there tears and bring back the Sharon I know." As I wiped my eyes, I managed to return her smile.

The first scheduled operation had been cancelled, due to an emergency in A & E. I was not happy. I had fasted from 12 o'clock midnight and they did not inform me of the cancellation until after 2 pm the following day. I had missed breakfast and lunch, and with all the medication, I felt very queasy and extremely hungry. It also meant that where I would have a full weekend to recover before Christmas, I now only had days, and the prospect of me being discharged before Christmas was now very unlikely.

Claude was on her way up to the hospital, as she wanted to be there before and after I went in for the operation and arrived just as they informed me of the cancellation; she was on a path to let heads roll. But as we debated about the inadequacies of the hospital, we finally deduced that there was a reason for all things, and we never know, perhaps that particular surgeon would have made a mistake and I could have encountered problems. We both ended up quoting, "In all things give God thanks because that is His will pertaining to you". 1 Thessalonians 5:18. We laughed, hugged and gave God thanks.

The operation was scheduled for the following Monday and went ahead as planned. Danny had arrived ahead of Claude.

When she walked into the room, I could see she was pleasantly surprised to see him seated on the bed with me. I did not mention the fact that he had only walked in a few minutes before her. I was glad they would both be waiting for me when I came out.

The WhatsApp group had been informed and everyone said they would all be praying. My friend Cora said she was going up to the Catholic church to pray and light a candle for me. Pastor had asked me to call her before I went in and with all the pre-op commotion, I completely forgot; she had called Claude's phone and she held it to my ear as Pastor prayed for protection, healing and a speedy recovery. I remember her adding that there was no distance in the Spirit; this meant the prayers were as powerful as if she was right there with me.

Once in theatre, all the required areas were numbed, and as the sedatives were administered I asked to be sedated as much as reasonably possible. Although extremely drowsy, I felt pain. At one time during the procedure, I screamed out for the surgeon to stop, as I felt him wrenching the device into a makeshift pocket in my flesh, just above my left breast. The surgical assistant gently mopped my brow as she calmly reassured me. Even whilst drowsy I could tell they were both relatively shocked at the level of pain I displayed and I had a high pain threshold. Once the device and leads were safely in place, the incision opening was sealed. The whole operation lasted almost three hours and I was fully awake the entire time.

Danny and Claude were both waiting for me when I returned to the ward. Although I have no recollection of our conversations; they tell me that I felt great under the circumstances and I had responded amazingly to the operation.

Thankfully the tests afterwards showed that there were no complications and the device was successfully programmed the following day in the pacing clinic. Dr Peters had informed us that it would be difficult to raise my left hand and I should attempt to raise it daily, a little bit at a time, to prevent it from seizing up. By the Wednesday, I was still very sore; the nurses were doing all they could to ensure that I could go home before Christmas. They checked the dressing for signs of bleeding, although it was not to be changed for a week. They made me very comfortable and assisted in every way possible, as I could hardly use my left hand.

Even though I was in my own room, I could sense a real buzz around the ward, as patients were happily being discharged and various staff were saying their goodbyes as they left for their holidays.

Dr Peters came in to see me. I was lying propped up on the bed; she took up her usual position at the end of the bed and picked up my notes. Smiling, she said, "We are really pleased with the operation. I know you felt some pain whilst it was going on, that's not the norm. How are you feeling now, Sharon?"

News travels fast, I thought.

"I'm fine, when can I go home?" I asked, eyes wide open and almost holding my breath.

"The heart seems to be functioning as expected and the device is working well. We need to monitor the swelling and if it goes down by tomorrow, as far as Cardiology is concerned, you can go home." She paused, as she seemed to be reading my notes, then continued. "Haematology will be taking blood samples this afternoon, and as far as I'm aware, if there are no issues, I can see no reason why you can't leave in the morning." Great, I thought and responded by saying, "Ok," without showing any optimism. She informed me that she would be working up to Christmas Day, so was available if I needed anything. "Anything at all," she emphasised, "and remember to keep that arm and shoulder moving gently. You don't want it to seize up." I couldn't wait to leave; many people had not expected me to leave the hospital alive. I was very open about my illness, the news was spread far and wide; and, as is typical when you hear the word 'cancer', negative news was going around that it was touch and go for me. Most of the time it was purely through what they had read about amyloidosis and myeloma, as the online prognosis was very negative, coupled with the testimony of those who had visited me and seen me in the worst possible state. I was determined to fight this disease, not be another statistic and certainly not follow my mother's footstep. I was not ready to leave my husband and children. As far as I was concerned, cancer is the small 'c' in my life. Jesus Christ is the big 'C'.

Chapter 20

HOME AT LAST

I was hurried out of hospital about 6 pm on Christmas Eve; the discharge had taken much longer than everyone had anticipated. After the doctors had visited me for the last time, at 2 pm, we were told that the discharge papers would follow shortly, within the next few hours. Danny arrived at 4 pm and made several trips to the car with my cases; we hadn't realised just how much baggage I had accumulated over the past six weeks. The delay to discharge me with all the medication and papers gave all my friendly nurses an opportunity to sit with me and sadly say their teary goodbyes, some truly believing that the next time they would see me would be in A & E, if at all.

Knowing that the only way I could leave the hospital and heart machines behind was with the implanted ICD left me with mixed feelings. Here I was, on my way home feeling worse than I felt before my admission six weeks before. Still unable to walk at any pace, out of breath and weakened by the chemotherapy and implant operation, I wanted to cry and give thanks at the same time. It was at this time that it really dawned on me just how much we take for granted. I struggled to make a cup of tea and sandwich; the six short steps from the kitchen sink to the fridge were now a challenge; all the ingredients had to be saved up on the side, so I would only have to make one trip to the fridge.

I was well aware that if I had not started the treatment, by now my heart would have been so attacked and damaged by the amyloid proteins it would have certainly packed up. Dr Willis had informed me that when the initial bone marrow tests were done, the light chains were in number 245, which gave a slight indication of the level of abnormal protein cells that were roaming around in my body and attaching themselves to my heart. After six weeks, with approximately one and a half cycles of chemotherapy, they were reduced to about 100; the chemotherapy was certainly working; however, the team had calculated that I would need at least eight cycles before they would be confident of killing all the abnormal cells.

Danny, me and my children spent Christmas and Boxing Day with Claude and her family. Normally we would have had his children, Chris, Tianna and Marcus, his brother Martin and sister Lorna Gee and anyone else who may have been on their own on Christmas Day. We loved cooking for the family and spending Christmas Day around the big family table; in fact, the year before we had fourteen seated for Christmas dinner.

At Claude's I was not allowed to do anything and quite frankly spent most of the time lying down. We had a wonderful time and I could see that everyone tried to make the most of the day; under the circumstances, it was difficult, with me on chemotherapy and the knowledge that the next dose would be due in a few days.

I would attend the day unit as an outpatient twice-weekly. On the first day I would have my blood tested and vitals taken; then Matt and the heart failure team would perform their examinations to ensure my heart was strong enough to receive and tolerate the chemotherapy the following day. Again new territory to me; I arrived at the day unit with other cancer patients, not knowing what to expect. It was one of the saddest experiences of my life. I was breaking up inside, my eyes watered, first for myself and then for every single patient who had their observations, tests and drugs administered. Everyone appeared so distraught, weak and frail; some with shaven heads, headscarves, steroid faces and novices, like me with wigs. The majority of us arrived by the hospital transport ambulances and were brought up to the unit in wheelchairs by the porters. I often thought that we were the people with the least time, yet our lives were taken up by waiting hours for the transport to pick us up, waiting hours for the drugs to be administered and waiting hours for the transport to take us home. It was literally an all-day affair. I observed that, for a lot of the patients, travelling in the ambulance was almost like a day trip, especially the elderly ones, who probably lived alone. Many brought a packed lunch, with the hope of meeting a fellow patient, to have a good chat with.

To kill time, I brought my iPad to read my kindle, or watch a pre-downloaded film, this seemed pointless after the first few times, as no sooner had I started watching a film, whether in the ambulance or unit, I would get chatting, make friends and exchange stories. Most of us on the ward had multiple myeloma and I even met one elderly man who had amyloidosis. Week after week, for eight months, we would come across the same patients and exchange and share our various stories. Although our stories were very different and we were all at various stages, of the illness, if we looked deeply enough in each other's eyes you would see the cloud which hung over our heads: one account that remained constant irrespective of duration of remission, the myeloma would always return, with a vengeance and no warning.

Visiting the ward weekly and meeting all the patients was very disheartening; I needed God's help to get the stories of doom and gloom out of my mind; I needed faith, first to believe that I would be cured and, although they call it remission, I had to believe that the chemotherapy would do what it needed the myeloma to do: go in remission and never return. I held onto the word in Isaiah 53:5 and repeated it daily: "But he was pierced for our transgressions, he was crushed for our iniquities; the punishment that brought us peace was on him, and by his wounds, we are healed."

Audrey and Winston checked up on me every day, they were exceptional and soon became very practical and emotional supporters. Things were not easy for them, particularly as Winston had had a leg amputated some years before. They hardly left my side. They both called me every day; if I was tired or lying down, Audrey would say, "Hush, mama take it easy." Together they started a trend and made a point of visiting us every Thursday; cooking me and the family a traditional meal, stew peas, Ackee and Saltfish, or oxtail with butter beans, being favourites. Before long, Thursday became the family day for me and my siblings (friends purposely stayed away). This period drew most of us closer together, especially Audrey and Winston.

I also had sporadic visits from Danny's friends and family. Some of my school friends from over 40 years before would visit (I hardly told Claude, as she was totally against visitors). My best schoolmates, Karen, Sammy and Lorraine, visited a few times during my treatment, usually on a Saturday, baking cakes, bringing gifts and sitting comfortably with me all day. We acknowledged that no matter how many years passed without seeing each other, we had not changed, there was still the schoolgirl secrets, giggles and stories to share. We had a mutual love which went back decades. We put it down to growing up in Brockley, South-East London, where there was a real community spirit. Everyone who knew us (The Brockleyites, as we called ourselves) commented that we were all like family and noted the affection and appreciation we displayed towards each other.

By August 2016 and eight cycles later, Dr Willis called me for my monthly consultation. The blood tests showed that the light chains were down to a safe level: they were under 30. They wanted to say that I had gone into remission, but until I had another bone marrow biopsy, they could not technically confirm. Claude was with me and we were so thankful, we knew the impending biopsy would confirm the remission.

I received the second bone marrow biopsy on the 12th of October 2016 and two days later received the confirmation from Pedro that I was definitely in remission. That weekend we celebrated Zack's 20th birthday and rejoiced and gave God thanks for my complete healing from myeloma.

Danny's father, who lived in Jamaica, was suffering from dementia and we had received news that he was deteriorating. Danny wanted to take me on a visit to finally meet him; however, we decided to see what Dr Peters thought about me travelling that distance.

Dr Peters' cardiology checks were not as encouraging. My first appointment with her after being told that the chemotherapy was successful left me rather disappointed.

My appointment was on the 20th of December 2016, just over a year since she had told me that my life expectancy was six months. She seemed genuinely pleased to see me. All the pleasantries were out of the way. (She always asked how Jess was, as she knew she was waiting for test results regarding her admittance to medical school.)

"So how are you feeling and getting on with the defibrillator?" she asked as she beckoned for Danny and me to sit down.

"No problems with the defib," I answered, "but I'm experiencing shortness of breath and struggling to go up the stairs." She listened intently as I continued. "Dr Peters, now that I'm in remission, surely my heart will go back to normal?" I asked, almost expecting a 'yes'.

"Sharon, imagine a heart that has had nuggets stuck to it day after day for a few years, making it stiff and quite hard in places. Just because one day you suddenly stop sticking the nuggets on it, the nuggets that are already in place do not automatically drop off. It can take years to repair: in some cases, they may never drop off."

I hadn't thought about it like that. Seeing the puzzled look on my face, she continued. "The chemotherapy's job is to stop the bone marrow from producing the abnormal light chains; however, it cannot repair the heart. Does that make sense?" she asked, eyes flitting from Danny to me.

"I guess so," I responded, looking at Danny. We had both expected that the heart would have repaired itself. I was never sure whether Danny's optimism was real or whether he said things for mere encouragement. Dr Peters was very clear and what she said made great sense, but Danny and I, true to form, refused to accept her diagnosis. We would continue to trust God for a new heart.

Chapter 21

THE WAITING GAME

With the myeloma in remission and my light chains down to a 'safe level', the Royal Free Hospital decided that my appointments could be annual; however, I was required to post bimonthly blood samples to them. This way they would check the light chains and monitor any changes. Initially getting the local hospital to take an extra vial of blood, (even though I provided the vial) was a challenge, most of the time I would be cross-examined to establish what my intentions were with the blood. I had to laugh as I thought, I really do not want to give any more blood than I have to, nor am I in the custom of selling blood. Eventually, I asked for a letter of explanation from the Royal Free, which helped most of the time.

The haematology appointments with Dr Willis were also bimonthly, to also monitor any changes with the light chains. They would check vitals, urine, and blood since from clinical experiences, as far as the professionals were concerned, it could be weeks, months or even years before the myeloma returned, but it would return. The cardiology and pacing clinic, which checked the device, would see me every six months. We had installed a Boston scientific heart-reading monitor, called

Latitude at home, which gave the heart failure team and pacing clinic remote access to monitor any failures and me the opportunity to send readings of my heart from the implanted device to the hospital at any given time.

The search engines were not subtle, I deliberately stopped myself from looking up the prognosis on google and had to make positive confessions. I repeatedly told myself that I would live for many years, to see my children graduate from university and exceed many more milestones. They needed me and I was grateful for every day that I lived to spend with them.

When Jess collected her final 'A' level results in August 2016, regretfully she had not received the required marks for Chemistry and therefore lost her conditional university place. The stress and uncertainty around the cancer had taken their toll on her, she was extremely stressed and clearly had not coped. Jess had made *me* her main concern; it was evident she was suffering from emotional trauma. She had contacted the university and was told that she would not have an opportunity to reapply to study Medicine, however, she could instead study Pharmacy as an alternative degree. This was not an option for Jess who, wanting to be a doctor all her life, was now totally devastated.

With my new lease of life, and with what I believed was my second chance to give Jess a second chance (ignoring the unwelcomed intervention from both Josh and Jess), true to form, I decided to approach the university on her behalf. Josh was dead set against it and told me not to bother to write to the university, as there was nothing they would do, and also it would only raise Jess's hopes in vain. Jess wouldn't discuss any more actions, as she was so distraught. When I had approached her, she was in bed with tears in her eyes, she said, "Just leave it, Mum, please." That was not an option for me. All their previous school admissions had been a fight. I knew how to write letters. After much prayer and deliberating with Pastor, I wrote to the Head of Admissions, with my mitigating circumstances and before long, we received news that Jess could re-sit her Chemistry exam and if she passed, would be given a place the following year. This was a fantastic achievement, as university students would not normally be given such an opportunity and certainly not at the same university. In disbelief and with jubilation, Jess studied hard and resat her Chemistry 'A' level.

In the meantime, I attended my various hospital appointments and tried my best not to be a cause for concern. It worked and by the 18th of August 2017, she received the 'A' she required and a subsequent place at one of London's top medical universities, UCL, to commence in October 2017.

Chapter 22

AUGUST 25TH, 2017 – OUR BILL

I woke up that Friday morning with an overwhelming feeling that I wanted to visit Bill in hospital. I saw Ron at Colin's funeral on Wednesday and he spoke to me openly. Ron was a friend of Danny's; more of a family friend, who had grown up with Danny's younger nephew. Both Ron and I were recovering from myeloma and we both anxiously looked to Bill for encouragement and inspiration; in fact, when I had had my first bone marrow biopsy in November 2015, it was a few years after Bill's first, he had asked me how it went and, although extremely painful, it was nothing like what he described, and as we shared stories I felt that we had two separate procedures; especially when Bill asked me if it was worse than childbirth! "It certainly wasn't," I replied and as I laughed, we both ended up in fits of laughter.

But I was laughing on the other side of my face a year later when I had the second biopsy. Lying on my side, the doctor had numbed my hip as much as she could with a local anaesthetic; however, this did not reach the bone where she was snapping her sample from. As she drilled into my side with a syringe and deeply sucked out a sample of my blood, I could not believe how excruciating the pain was, I was in tears; Danny was there squeezing my hands, then Jo my Macmillan nurse also came in and tried to calm me down by soothingly rubbing my leg. She was a friendly face but I couldn't help thinking what was so different this time that I needed so much assistance, and whether something was going wrong.

Twenty minutes had passed, but it seemed like an hour. The pain was now unbearable, I was screaming and shouting in agony, but the worst was to come. The doctor was apologising for the pain and explained that the first part of the procedure was over and she was now drilling into the centre of the bone in an attempt to clip the marrow. Jo was telling me to take deep breaths, I was shaking my head in disbelief, another twenty minutes had passed and just as I was about to throw up, the doctor hastily reported that it was all done. My immediate thoughts were of Bill and what he had asked about childbirth and all I could do was agree; after experiencing three natural births, I concluded that this pain was so much more intense. While the doctor dressed the wound, I was advised to remain on the bed for a further fifteen minutes and when I was permitted to leave, I left the hospital limping and needed paracetamols for the pain.

I called Bill to share the experience. He was in Jamaica, where he had returned after his stem cell treatment and chemotherapy. "I need that vitamin D," he had explained. WhatsApp seemed to be playing up, so I ended up texting him, explaining it all in great detail. I made sure to tell him it was worse than ever, yes worse than my excruciating childbirth experience. I ended on a cheery note by telling him it's over now and he texted back: 'Oh gosh, hush!' That said it all: I knew he had felt my pain.

I needed and relied on Bill so much. He checked in with me frequently, even whilst he was recuperating in Jamaica; we made sure we knew where each other was at, in progress. He often said he was three years ahead of me with the myeloma. We were so delighted when he had made it to our wedding: he had just completed cycle four out of six of his chemotherapy treatment and thankful that this was his chemotherapy-free week. Bill danced through his pain and whilst we didn't want him to leave, we could see he was tired and could take no more.

As soon as I was up, I asked Danny what his schedule was like, as I wanted us to visit Bill and, although he was quite busy, he said morning would work better for him. We were set to leave after breakfast, which I was about to cook. That was until Danny and I started a silly argument about a pile of paper left on the dressing table. It was a trivial, ridiculous argument, which left me walking out of the house. I had no intention of visiting Bill alone, so I drove to my nearest Waitrose, some ten minutes away, for a free coffee and an iced Danish bun. Feeling better, I rang Danny to say it wasn't about us, but Bill, and I was on my way back. I wasn't sure whether I wasn't listening, or couldn't hear what he was saying and just assumed that he said ok.

On returning to the house, I found it empty, so I called Danny to find out where he was. It was now 1 pm and I really wanted us to leave sooner rather than later. He said he was ten minutes away. I waited at the end of the drive and as he pulled up I instinctively went to open the door, to jump in, but he beckoned for me to wait. He stepped out of the car and silently walked me back up the drive and into the house. My gut was hurting. Once inside he let out the shrillest cry I had ever heard from a man. I knew immediately it was Bill. We were too late. Apparently, he had had a slight seizure the night before and by 12:00 the following noon he was gone. Danny and I both made our way into the front room, where we slumped on the sofa and bawled, trance-like. We held each other and continued to weep: there were no words. Our best friend was gone.

The sting of losing Bill was so great; I am choked up and numb. I still cry for him some days; although he was ill, nothing prepared us for this loss; it was magnified, it was twofold, we had lost a dear friend and also a fellow sufferer who knew my pain and gave me hope and encouragement. This feeling of loss and deep emptiness could never be filled.

Being able to provide catering for both the traditional 'Nine Night' and the funeral was an honour, which kept Danny distracted and very busy. He went all out for our Bill and I supported him wherever I could. It was our own special tribute, just how he would have wanted it. Bill had given me such hope of beating this disease; I knew I now had to muster every single being in me to fight my own battle.

I have to finish this book: for Bill and all the positivity and hope he represented, for the matchless love I'm so grateful to have received and passed on: and for my children, to read a little part of my history (When Jess read a little of my story, she once exclaimed, "Wow, Mum, you had 'a life' before us.")

Chapter 23

TODAY, AGAINST ALL ODDS

I am living with reduced mobility, as they say, 'a shadow of my former self'. I'm envious (in a good way) when I see people dancing. I loved to dance, even though my children would tease me, saying I have no rhythm. In my mind I was still that teenager who danced to soul in the 80s, nicknamed 'My flexible friend' from an Access credit card advert at the time; if only my children could have seen me then.

As an adult, I had had ballroom dancing classes. Danny and I had taken salsa classes for a while and still hope that one day I would be able to dance again.

I feel emotional when my husband asks me to visit the gym with him, seeing his disappointment when I say, "I can't." Although the myeloma has been in remission since August 2016, there is the ongoing cardiac amyloidosis (Mayo stage 2), where I bear the pressure on my heart with each step I take. It is painful for me, knowing that I needed no invitation in the past, would be the first to instigate a gym or swim session with him, on top of all my various classes. Now apart from the infrequent slow swimming sessions, I have no stamina or energy to visit the gym.

A day does not pass without me thinking about my sister Viv, my mother, Papa G, Phil and Bill, as well as my numerous friends and family that I have lost over the years. I take comfort from having known such great people, and give thanks for having experienced their idiosyncrasies in my life.

Since my discharge from hospital, to help improve hospital cancer care I have joined St George's focus group, strategy group and even helped to make a video for post-cancer care, whilst giving feedback through talks and sharing my experiences. I have volunteered at my church and plan to assist wherever I can to make a difference to those around me.

After the treatment had finished, Claude hastily decided that we would all have a family holiday in Rhodes. With us came Zack, Jess, Audrey, Dr Jacky, Michelle, her husband Ciaran, and my two nephews, Sanchez and Jacob; it was truly a holiday to remember and another book. Danny and I visited Seville and finally Jamaica, where even though my travel insurance was more than double the flight, we had a great time and it was well worth it. I have determined in my heart to live the best life that I physically could. For Claude's 50th birthday nine years ago, Annie and her husband Steve, took us skiing in Courchevel and wants us to accompany them again for Claude's 60th. There was at least ten of us. Courchevel is absolutely picturesque, but Skiing is not my forte, even with dry ski slope lessons beforehand, this was one sport I did not master. I failed to see how anyone could enjoy a holiday where so much baggage had to be lugged around each day. We had a hilarious time, with stories that Steve continually divulges at parties: especially one where I came down a slope on his back. It's now time to make that decision again and I may just take her up on it: no skiing of course!

With my primary schoolmate Alan (Big Al) we have already organised a couple of small primary school reunions, in between my sicknesses. We had previously met up at Colin's funeral, a dear friend whom we had both grown up with. Colin was a good ten years younger than us and we were all touched by his story and subsequent death.

"We have got to stop meeting like this, under these dismal settings, life is too short," Alan said, as we both walked out of the church after the service. I knew exactly what he meant: the funerals were getting too frequent and unbearable; the younger the person, the more it impacted our feelings. He was aware of my condition and I responded. "Yes, when we meet up with our friends, we just want to have a laugh. It's so difficult under these circumstances." We both agreed and that is where the idea of a Brockley reunion was birthed. A few months later, about twenty-five of us met for a small Christmas, reunion dinner in the Croydon Park hotel. Months later, Alan and I organised a small reunion party, with sixty of us, in the function bar at Club Langley; Danny prepared a lovely buffet and we danced to the sounds of 5th Avenue. Although we were hoping for a larger turnout, it was great meeting up with old friends, under lovely settings. Alan is still on my case to help organise the 'Big one.'

In the clinic, at my most recent haematology appointment, Dr Willis gave me a huge hug, as I shared with her my enthusiasm for completing my story; with her smiling eyes, she encouraged me, saying, "It's so important to hear positive stories, especially with the myeloma survival rate being so low, not many people have an opportunity to share their story or live to tell the tale. I would certainly promote your book."

I had made quite a few names in my book, fictitious, but Dr Willis insisted that I use her real name, and said, almost as if reminding me, "We were with you, on that journey, all the way. Who would have thought you would be here today?" She paused, shaking her head and continued. "The saddest part for me was when you so innocently and proudly showed me your beautiful wedding photos and there and then, I realised you and Danny were only recently married."

Yes, our wedding was quite fresh at the time and having my laptop in the hospital with me, I would proudly show the team many pictures; a kind of 'before and after' illustration. I appreciated Dr Willis so much. She was clearly saddened at the time; however, she never let on. I knew that all of the professionals and most friends were baffled at my progress and obvious development.

Shocked by my tolerance and calmness, I am often asked why I do not pursue a negligence case against the first hospital, who was ignorant of my symptoms. "After all, you were under their care for over eighteen months, with no diagnosis," my friend Karen had said. "And if you had not chosen St. George's, we all know you would not be here today." I knew this sentiment was echoed by many, and although the clinicians do not always provide a right diagnosis; I share my story for individuals who may not know how to fight.

My story is to build awareness and to urge clinicians to do more, to be more mindful and perceptive of symptoms that clearly alert them to our rare or complicated conditions. Misdiagnosis being a soaring, massive and all too frequent problem. In my case, there were clear 'alarm bells'. Somehow I cannot move on from this point without mentioning D'lissa, my friend's young daughter, who sadly passed away in childbirth and left behind her baby daughter, S'riaah severely brain-damaged from birth and living with cerebral palsy. Perhaps only a short questionnaire could have saved her life, again another story.

Whilst one hospital got it very wrong and almost cost me my life; another completely saved me. I am in no position, physically or mentally to take on a battle. My battle is to stay alive.

I now trust God for my complete healing. Although cardiac amyloidosis comes with a poor prognosis, irrespective of all of this and the negative comments of my heart failure team, I know God has healed my heart and so far has a plan for my life. As the end of Isaiah 53:5 says, "….By His stripes, we were healed". Therefore, if I was healed, then I am healed.

I am so thankful for my life; I'm celebrating all that God has done for me. Each year that I live is a blessing. So far, in just a few years, I have had the opportunity to really get to know my friends again, be a source of encouragement to many friends and family and be inspired even more, in return. I have seen so many changes in the lives of my children and had the opportunity to support and love them deeply; I have been able to live and see life in such a different yet beautiful way. I deeply breathe in the fresh air each day and give praise to God.

I could have thrown the towel in, given up and succumbed to what the professionals and my prognosis dictated, but I did not. I am fighting as hard as I can because I know that 'what is impossible with man is possible with God'. Mustard seed faith always at the ready.

My parents left a great legacy, twelve children (I still cannot exclude Viv from this number), 39 grandchildren, 59 great-grandchildren, and 4 great-great-grandchildren. My story briefly touches upon my family and friends, really just the tip of an iceberg, there is so much more to be told.

More than anything else, *Why Me?* shares my experiences and highlights two rare conditions, multiple myeloma and amyloidosis, which threatened my whole existence. Our natural tendency, as sufferers, is to retreat, hide the fact, go quiet, even cease communication with our friends; but I needed to speak up. As Dr Willis put it, "A voice for those who had no words."

Why Me? Inspired by the biblical story in St. John, chapter 9: about a blind man. Jesus responded, saying, "neither this man nor his parents sinned, why he was born blind, it's so that the works of my Father in Heaven may be made manifest in him."

That's why *I say* with great conviction, "I am healed, so that the works of *my Father* in Heaven may be made manifest in me."

Why Me? I reply, "Why not Me?"

- - - THE END - - -

Acknowledgements

First and foremost, I thank God, my Saviour, whose guidance and grace enabled me to confidently complete and publish my first memoir: *Why Me?, an*d whose strength has carried me through every step.

To my wonderful children, Joshua, Zachary and Jess, you have been my backbone. To my beautiful siblings, all of you are very dear to me: Jenny, Pat, Polly, Michael, Joan, Audrey, Claudette, Juliet, Elaine and Paul, as are your partners and my nieces and nephews.

To my Pastors, Dr Curdell McLeod and Pastor Herby McLeod, your prayers and guidance have been invaluable. I am grateful to my friend, Dr Jacqueline McLeod, whose support predominantly inspired Chapter 4, *A Friend who Sticks Closer than a Sister.*

To three very special ladies, who encouraged me to write: Joan Morgan, I was a young single mother and you were my Psalmody student over 20 years ago, I shared my poetry with you and you saw something in me that led you to constantly encourage me to write, never giving up on me. Bev Lee, always perceptive, quietly influential, and a steadfast, loyal friend.

Raye Henry, more recently, encouraged and pushed me to keep going and finish my book. "Are you there yet?" was the push I needed to complete my book.

To my friends and family who read my unfinished manuscripts, commented on photos or layout, I am so fortunate to have such talent in my midst: Bev, Claude, Syreeta, Jacky, Ingrid, Sharon Nelson, Raye and Sonia, your critique and advice have been invaluable. Thank you.

If you have offered encouragement or support throughout my journey, even if your name has not been mentioned, please believe that my gratitude lies deep within my heart.

I am truly blessed and thankful to have amazing family and friends, *without you all, this dream would have remained just a dream.*

Finally, to my Publishers, Douglas Walker and Frances Prior-Reeves, thank you for your patience and for making this intricate work of publishing uncomplicated, helping me bring *Why Me?* to life.

Dedicated to the Memory of:
My parents: *Mr George Ferdinand Phillips and Mrs Cotcheta Maria Phillips*
My beloved sister: *Mrs Vivienne Rachel Townsend*
The late great: *Mr Phillip Linton & his father*
My Father-in-law: *Mr Harold Linton*
My dear friend: *Mr William (Bill) March*
My Mother-in-law: *Mrs Euphemia Hamilton*
Leroy's father: *Mr Aston Cole (Grandad)*
And to all my other precious family and friends, gone on before (unfortunately too many to name),
Always in my heart

Family christening 1969

Back row: Kenneth, Sydney, Paul, (late Dad) Papa G, Viv, Polly, Mike, (late cousin) Oliver Marsh

Middle row: (late) Tiny Burke, Claude, Polly's baby Yvonne, Deon (partly hidden)

Front row: Elaine, Pam, Juliet, me, (late) Tony Finnikin, Derek.

John Stainer – My primary school

Excuse me for not remembering all the names
(it was over 45 years ago)

Back row: Nicola, me, Pat, Karen, Donna, ?, Brenda, Mr Jones

Middle row: ?, ?, Norman, Errol, Dave, Richard, ?

Front row: ?, Mustafa, ?, ?, ?,?, Denzel, Alan (big Al)

Me age 16

In my parents front room:
There are two sculptured heads on the cabinet made by (late Dad) Papa G

Me age 23

Me aged 18

In our Front room at home

Getting ready to go out

(Late) Mum – 1940s

(Late Dad) – Papa G – 1940s

Mum & (Dad) Papa G with Josh at Viv's wedding – 1992

Mum & (Dad) Papa G with me and eight sisters – Dad's 70th – 1993

My beautiful (late) Sister Viv

Viv & me, New Jersey – 1983

Viv & me,
Empire State Building – 1983

Me & Viv,
London – 1994

(Late) Phil Linton

Phil with Jess – 1997

Phil 2000

Phil with Zack – 1997

Phil with Josh &
baby Zack – 1996

Day out riding in Chipstead, Surrey

Danny, me, Jesse, Tianna, Marcus & Chris

Lorna Gee (receiving an award) and me at the awards ceremony – 2013

Our family: all grown up

Tianna, Marcus, me, Danny, Chris

Josh, me, Jess, Zack

Our Wedding day

Leaving St. Peter's church after the ceremony

Our wedding dance

My children: Jess, me, Zack & Josh

Our wedding day

My siblings

Back row: Mike, Claude, Juliet, Elaine, Paul

Front row: Polly, Joan, me, Pat, Jenny, Audrey

Claude & me

Our Honeymoon, Morocco – 2014

Boston 2008

Zack & Jess at Harvard

Me by the Charles River in Boston

The children and me in Boston

Zack and Me – 2014

Bickles Restaurant

Danny & me serving customers

Me & Danny opening day

Me serving Viv Richards (cricketer, who returned to Bickles for our braised oxtail)

Jerking chicken at the Hootananny, Brixton

Outside Bickles on a Brixton 'Splash' day

Our final day at Bickles

Week 2 in hospital –
chemotherapy kicking in

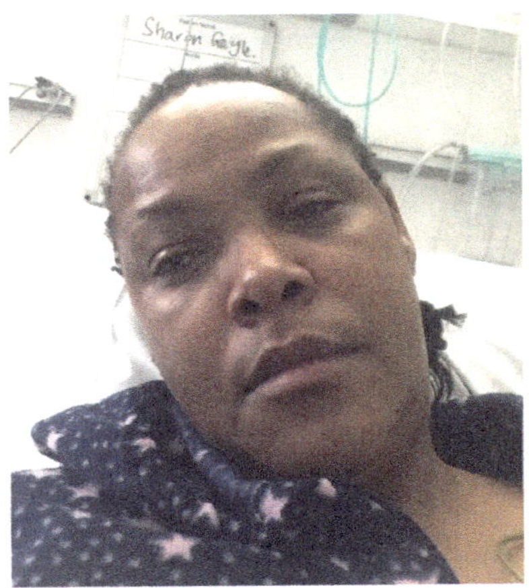

Peter my daily phlebotomist
at St. George's hospital

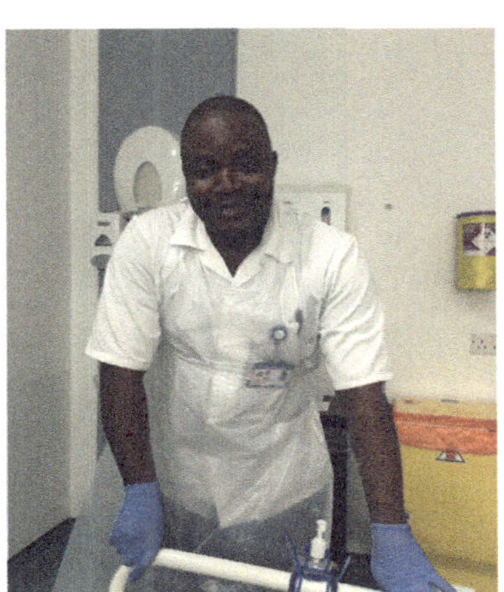

Jess & me in Rhodes – 2016
steroids have taken their toll

Out of hospital –
kisses from Jess

In Loving Memory

Vivienne Townsend
January 22, 1954 to September 1, 1996

Viv's Wedding Day, USA

Me, cousin Monique, my sister Joan, Viv, Vern, best man Ron and (Denzel's brother) David Washington

Made in the USA
Coppell, TX
08 October 2025

61032468R00098